RHAPSODY IN BLUE

FOR SOLO CLASSICAL GUITAR

Arranged by ANTHONY D'ADDONO

For more information on Anthony D'Addono visit: www.tonydaddono.com

ISBN 978-1-4768-7250-9

7777 W. Bluemound Rd. P.O. Box 13819 Milwaukee, WI 53213

Visit Hal Leonard Online at
www.halleonard.com

Rhapsody in Blue

By George Gershwin
Arranged by Anthony D'Addono

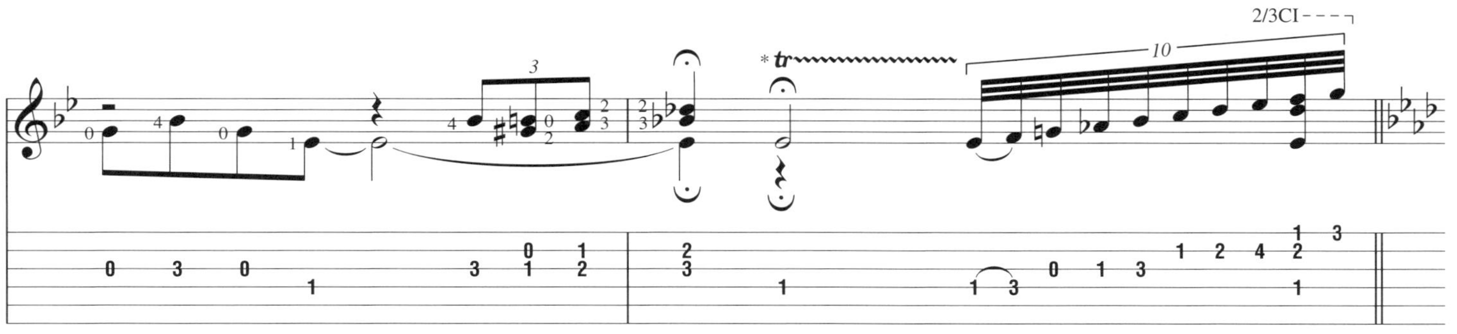

*Alternate L.H. hammer-on and pull-off with R.H. hammer-on and pull-off

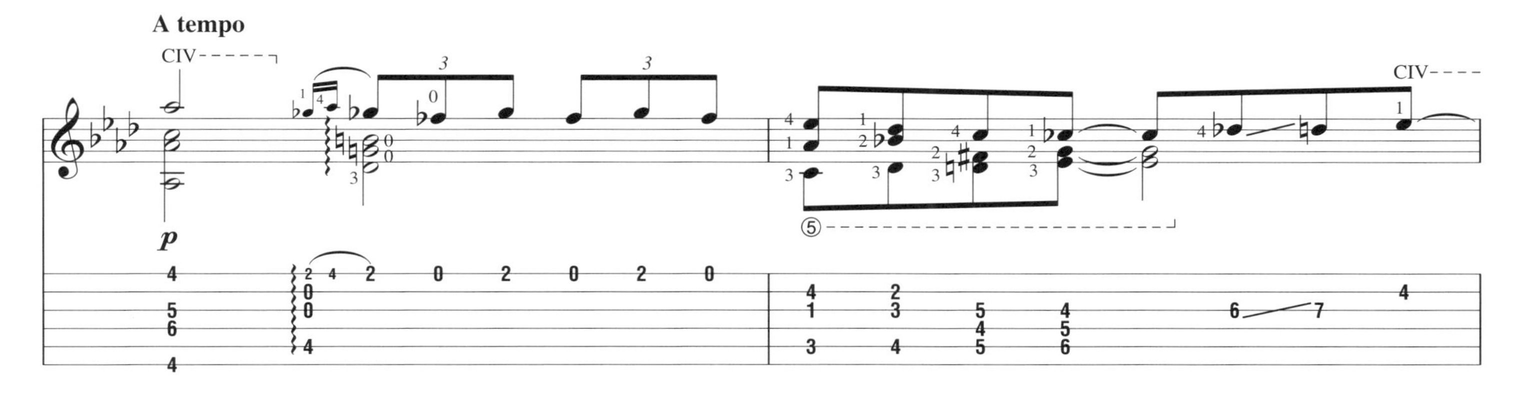

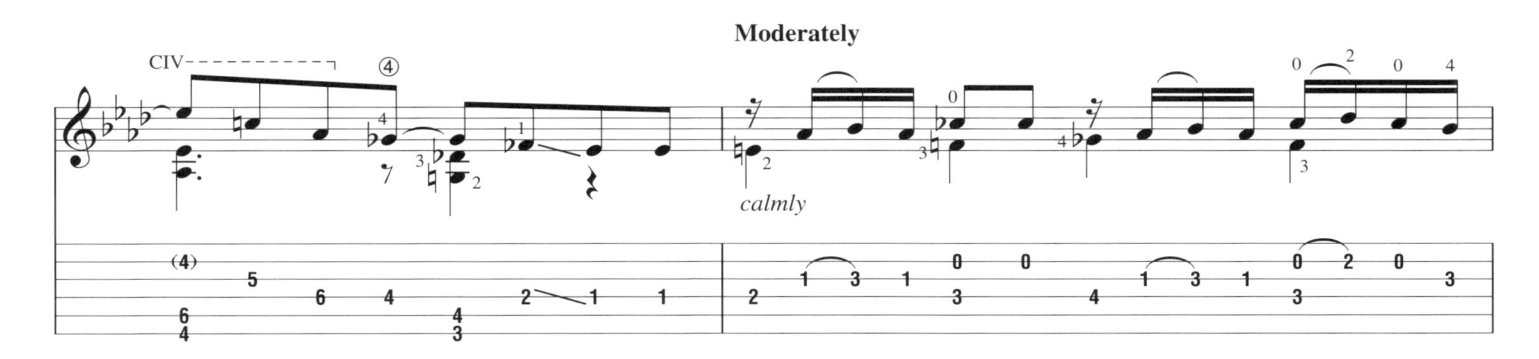

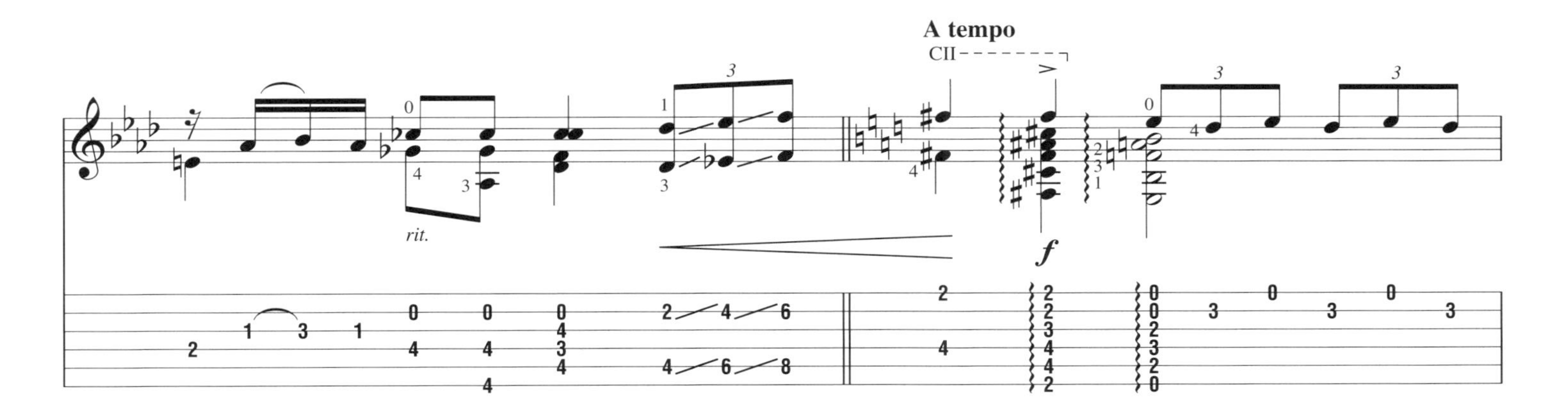

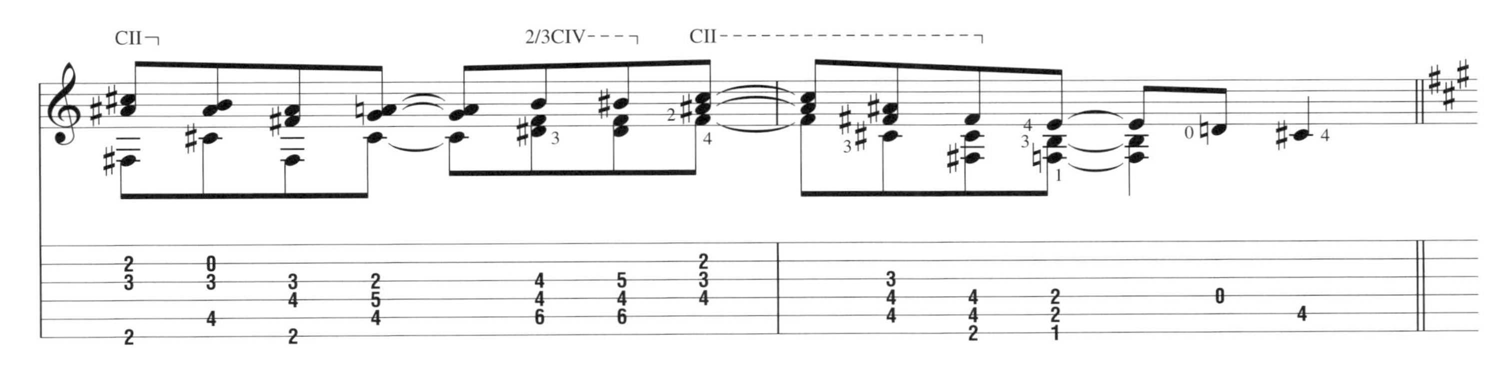

1/2CVII
playfully
Slower
5/6CIII
*sul ponticello
*Pick strings near bridge.
A tempo
Harm.
Harm.
1/3CXII
1/3CX
1/3CVIII

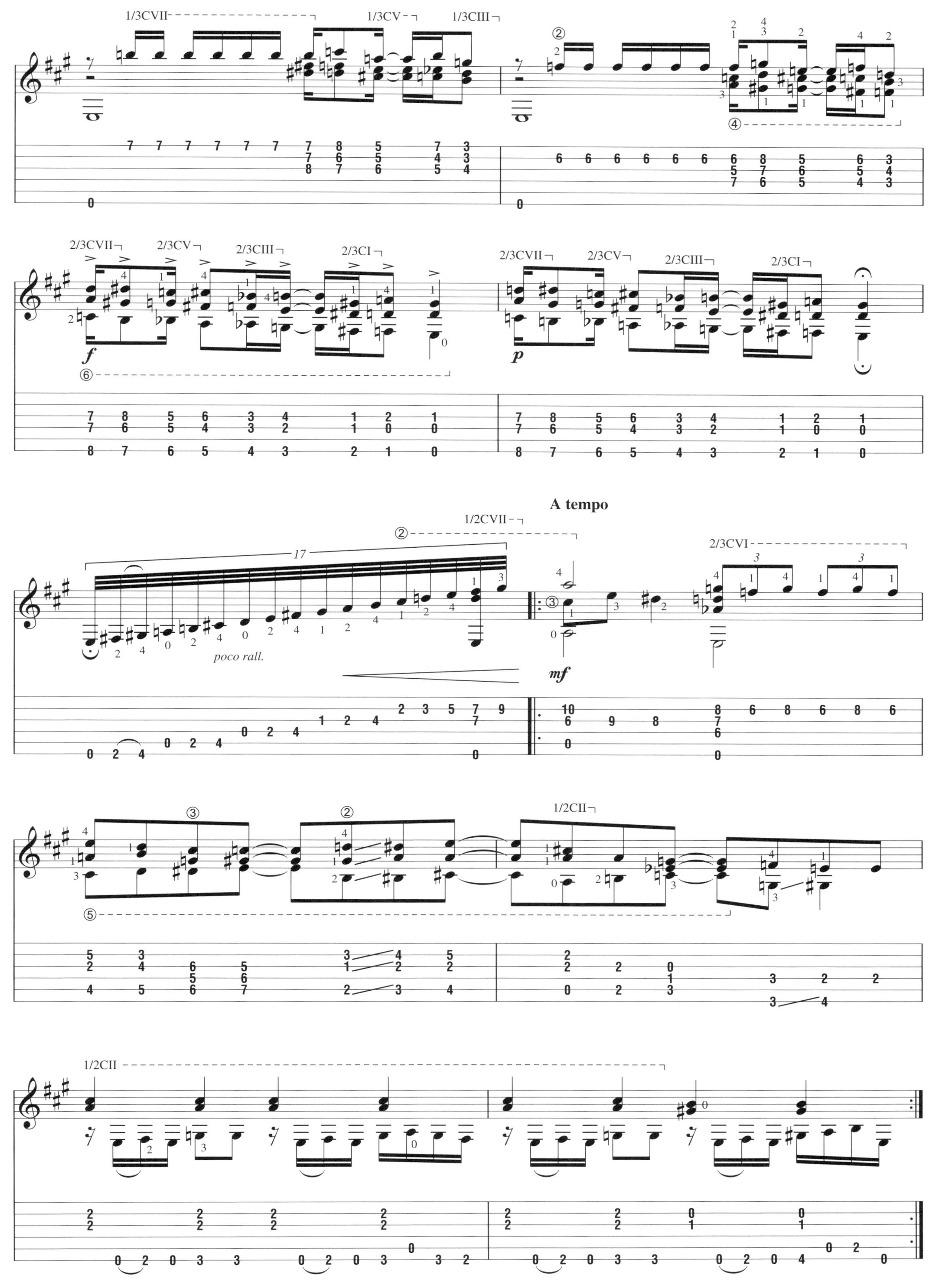
1/3CVII
1/3CV
1/3CIII
2/3CVII
2/3CV
2/3CIII
2/3CI
f
p
A tempo
1/2CVII
17
poco rall.
2/3CVI
mf
1/2CII

calmly

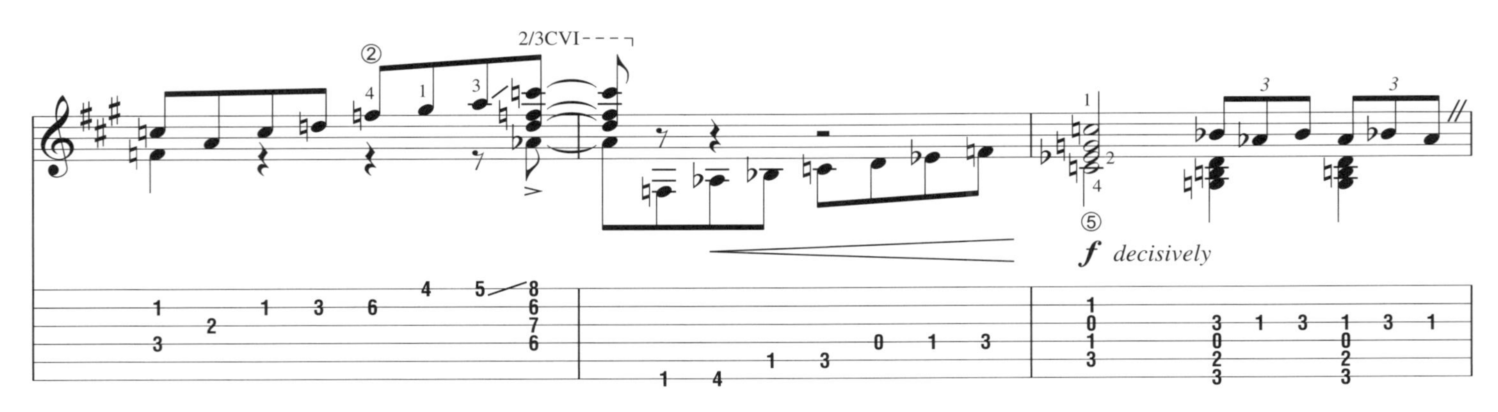
2/3CVI
f decisively

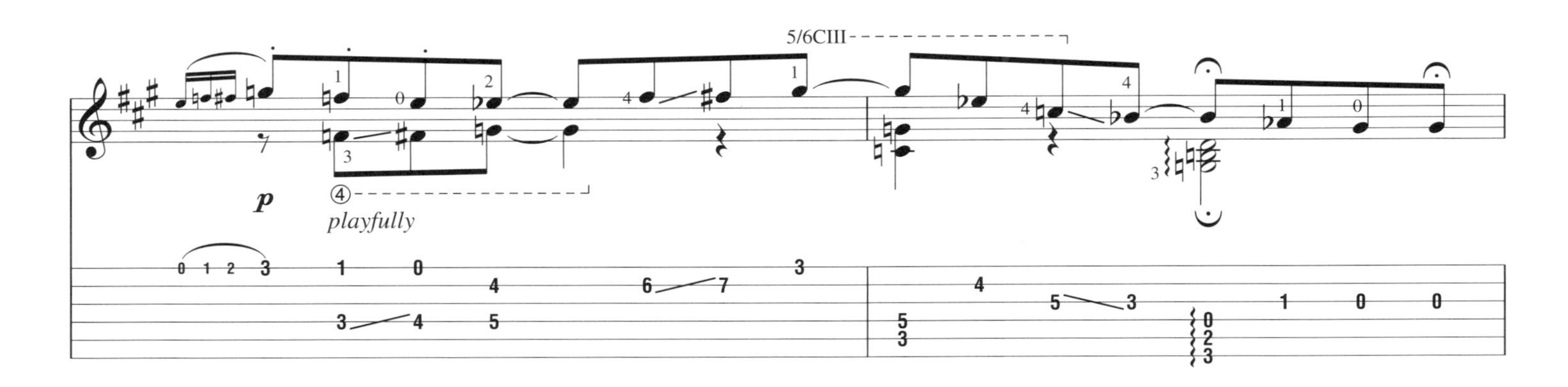
5/6CIII
p
playfully

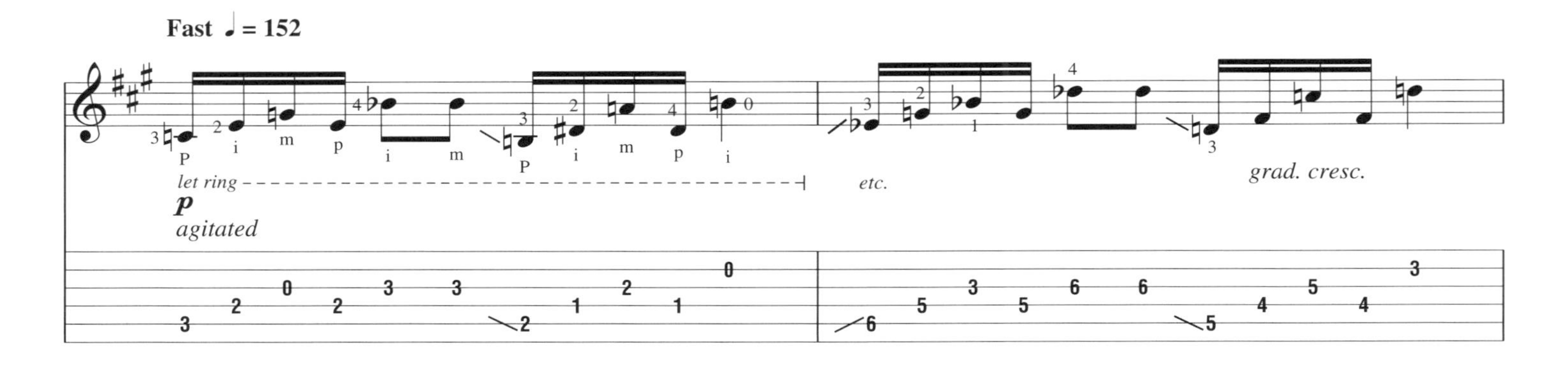
Fast ♩ = 152
let ring
p
agitated
etc.
grad. cresc.

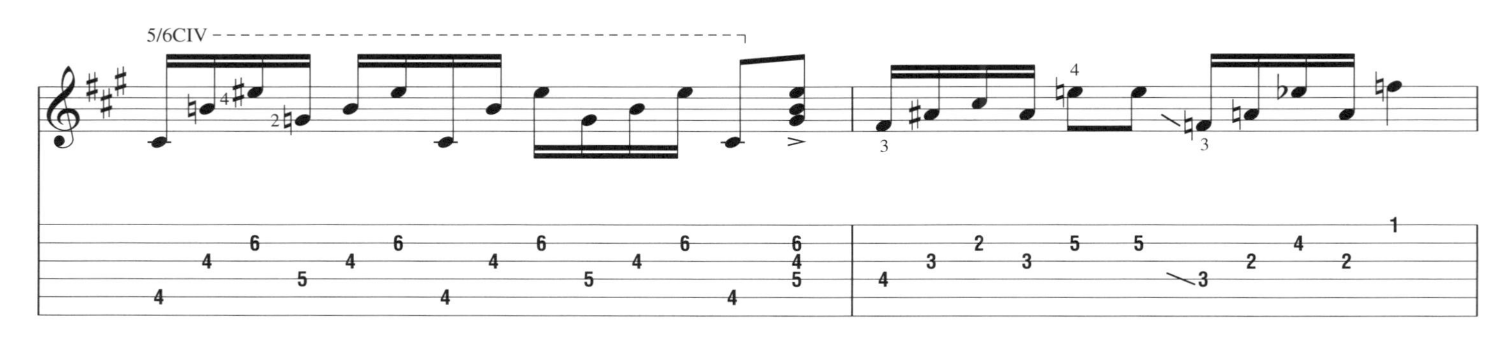
5/6CIV

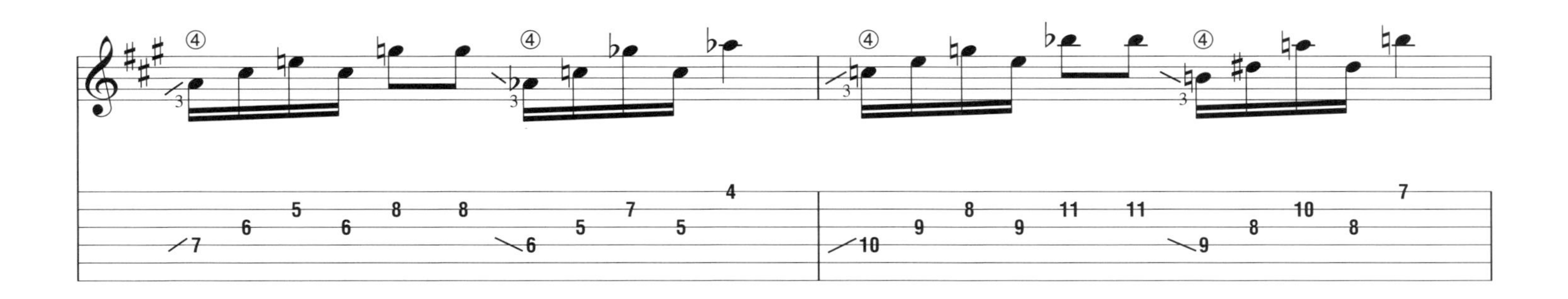

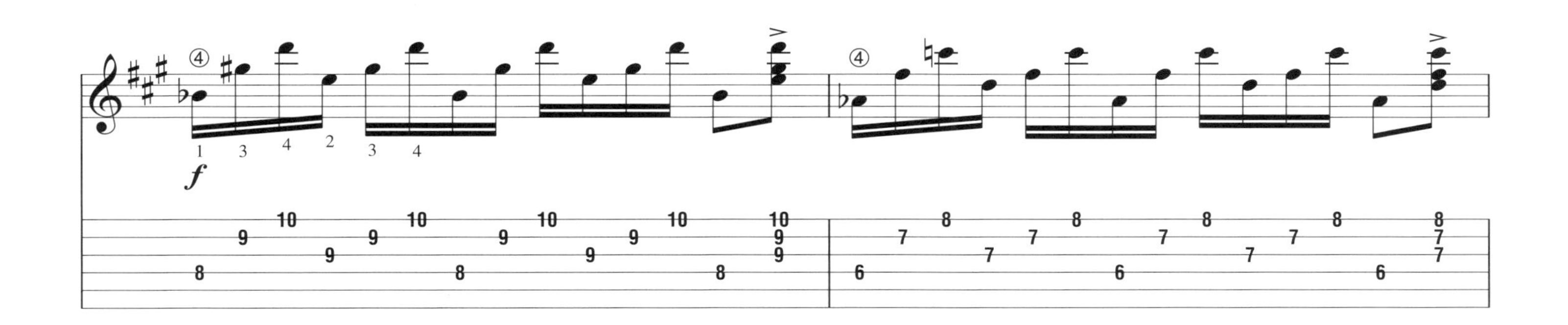

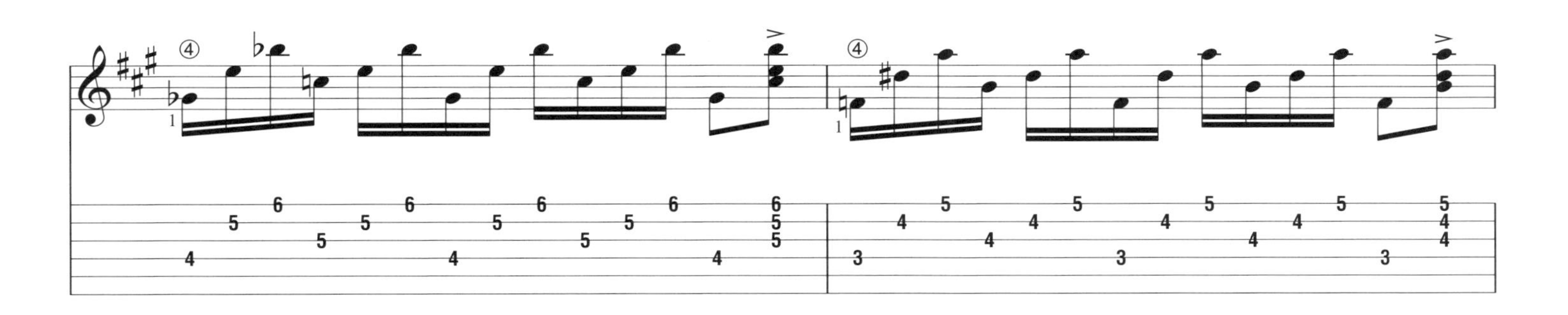

Moderately ♩ = 104
Harm.

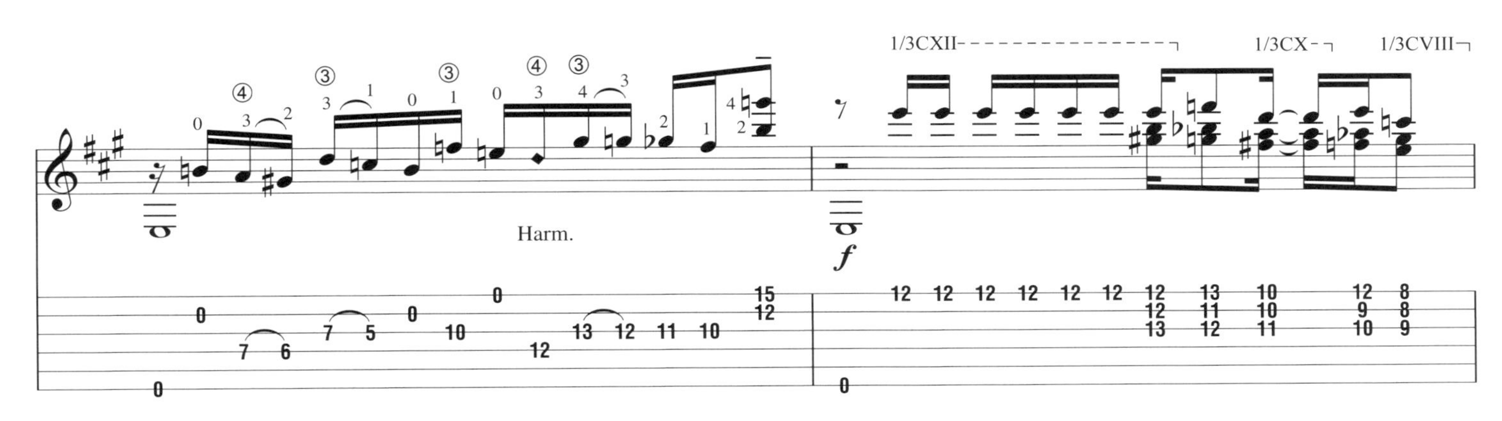
1/3CXII
1/3CX
1/3CVIII
Harm.

1/3CVII
1/3CV
1/3CIII
Moderately fast ♩ = 144
2/3CII
poco rit.
steadily
1/2CII
2/3CII
1/2CII
2/3CII

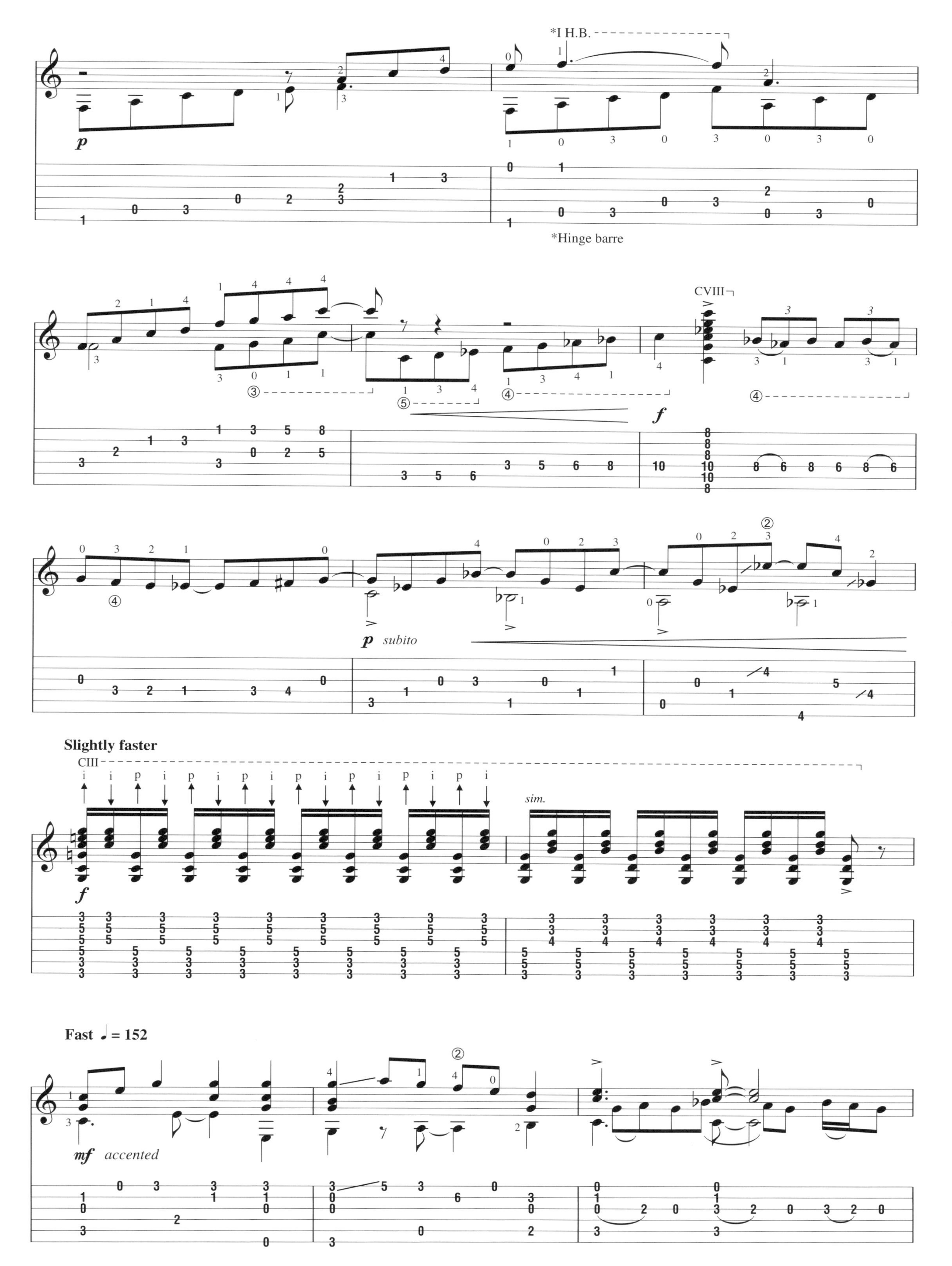
*I H.B.
*Hinge barre
CVIII
p subito
Slightly faster
CIII
sim.
Fast ♩ = 152
mf accented

*Harp Harmonic: The note is fretted normally and a harmonic is produced by gently resting the right hand's index finger 12 frets (one octave) above the indicated fret while the right hand's ring finger assists by plucking the appropriate string.

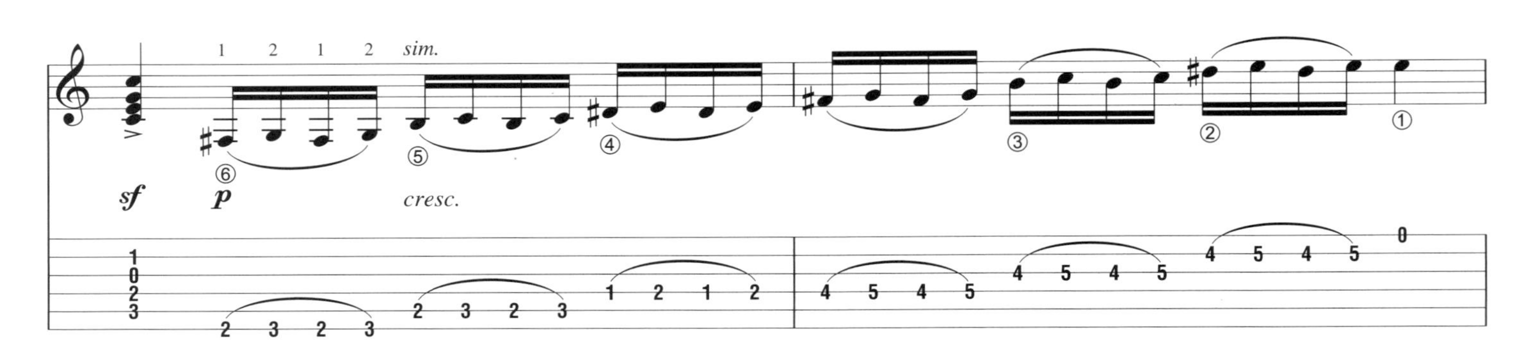

CV
sim.
cresc.
CII
rall.
A tempo ♩ = 152
CIII
CIII
CIII

CIII
CIII
CI
CI
p
CI
mf
Slower
p
i m i m
Harm.
p
i m
Harm.
rit.

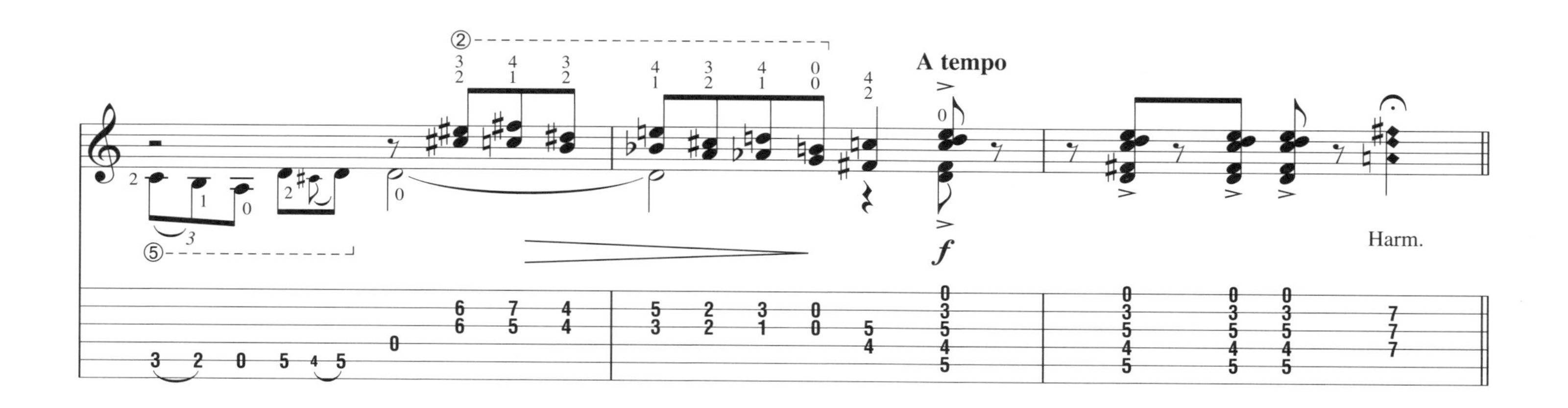

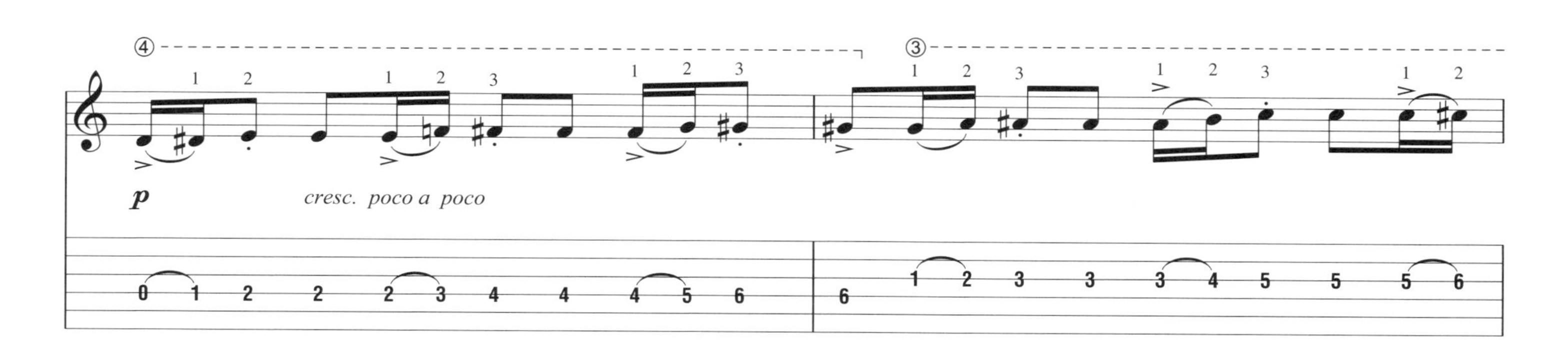

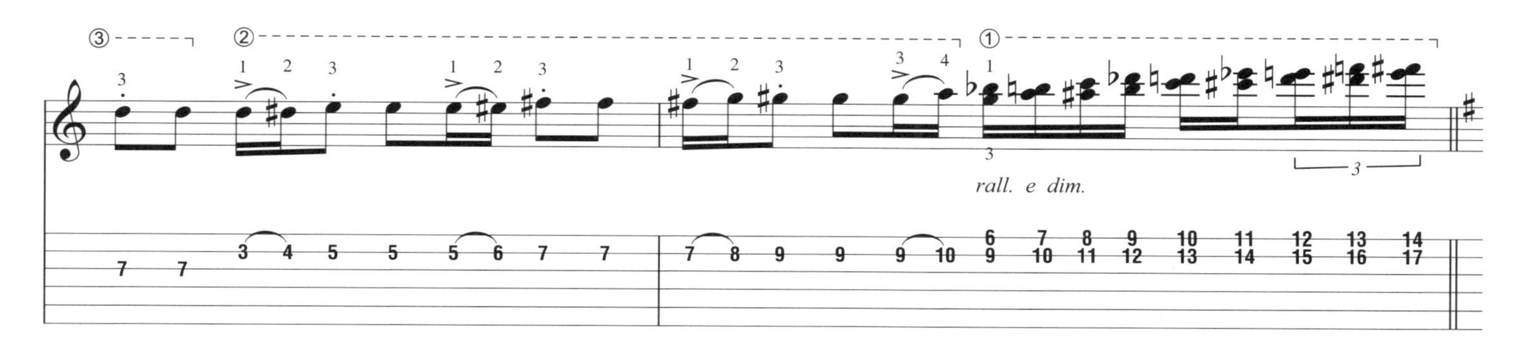

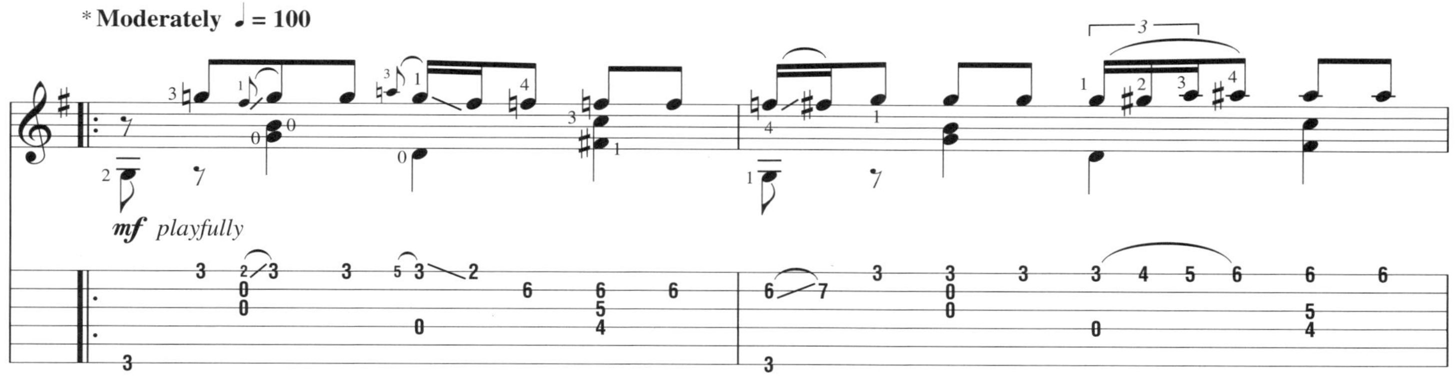

*Tempo should fluctuate with the rise and fall of the melody.

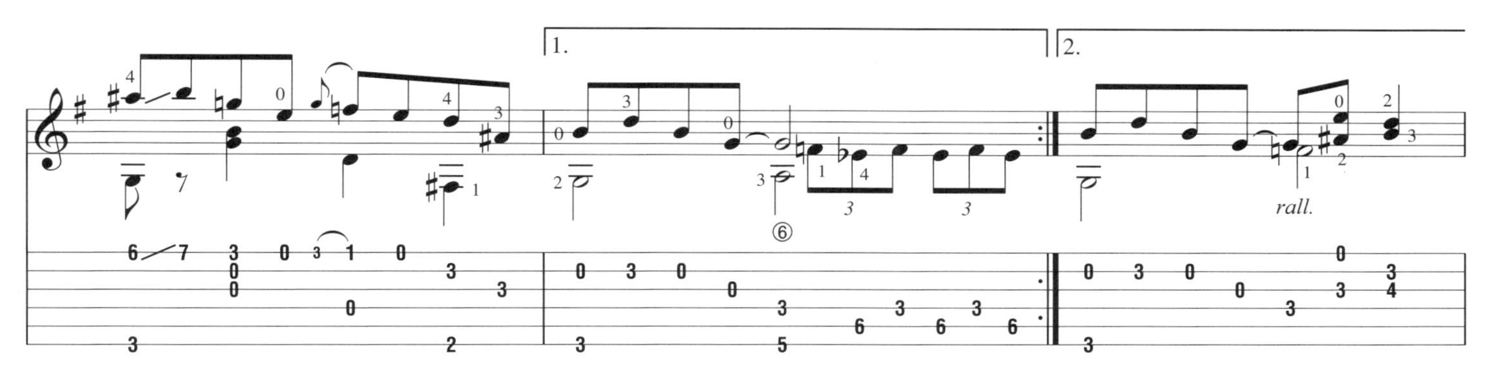

1/2CVIII
accel.
1/2CVIII
A tempo
rall.
Moderately slow ♩ = 92
1/2CII

1/2CVII
1.
2.
Faster
*IX
VII
IV
II
p playfully
rall.
*Position indications, next 3 meas.
IX
VII
IV
II
rall.
A tempo
1/2CII
rall.
1/2CVII

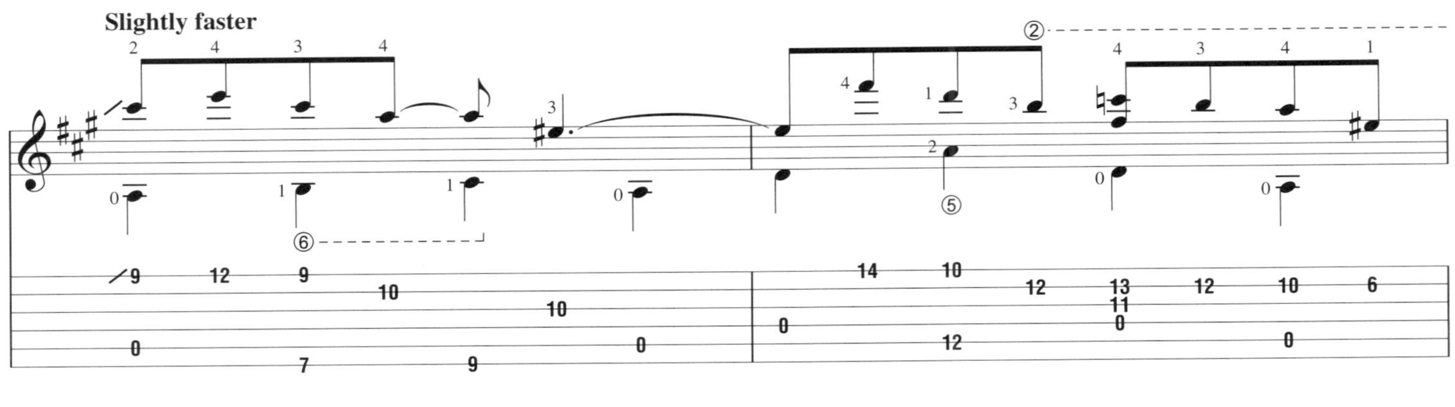

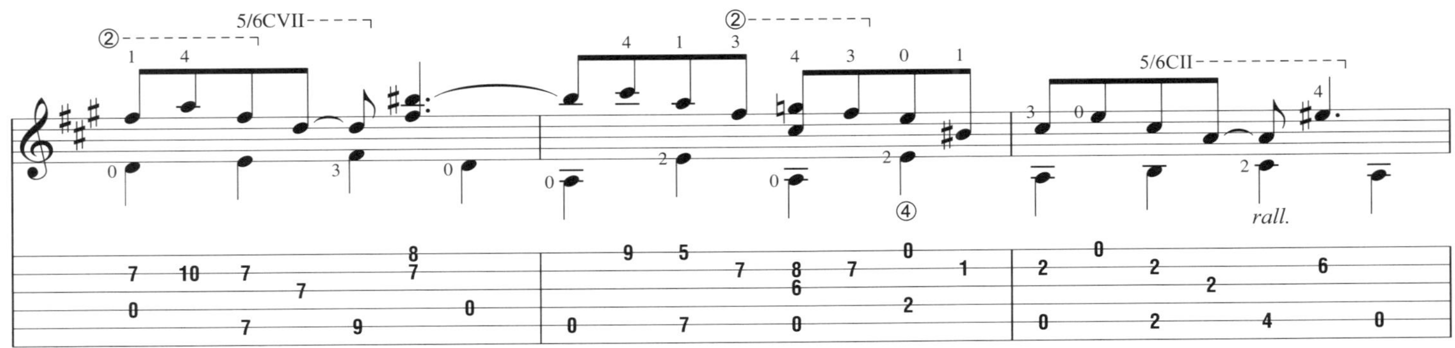

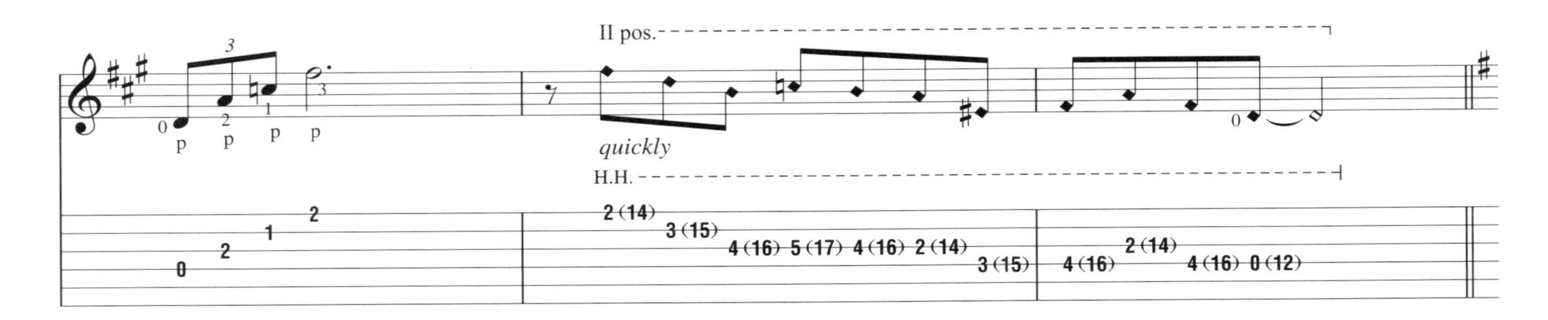

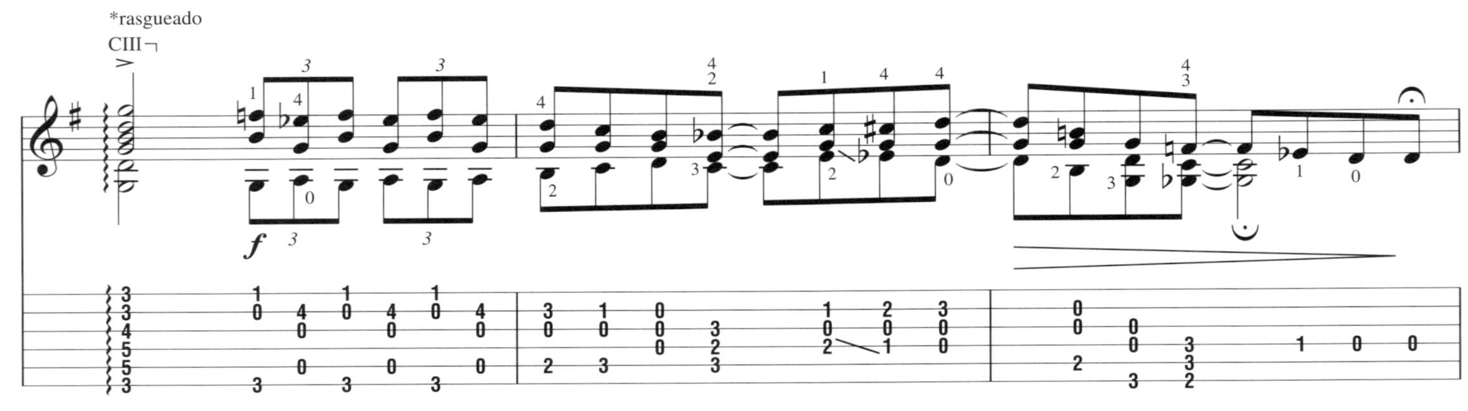

*Strum strings using multiple fingers in quick succession.

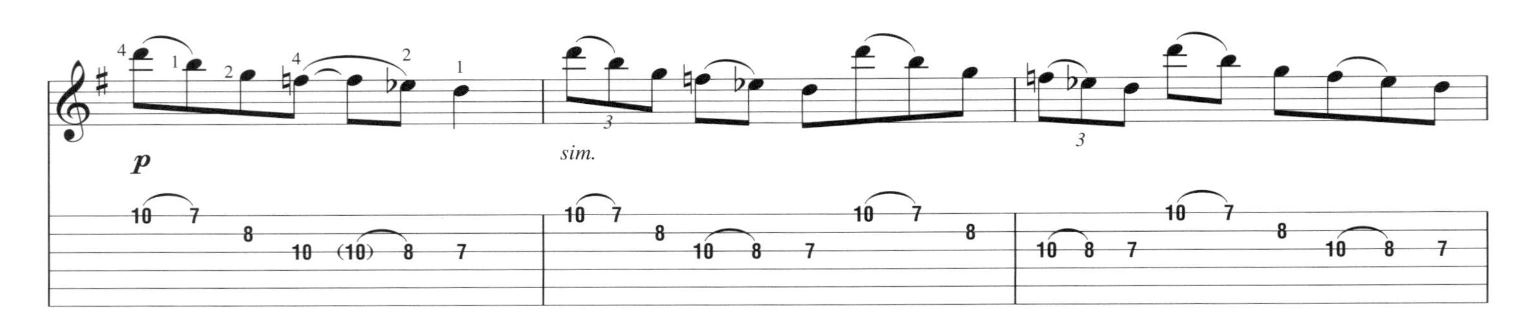

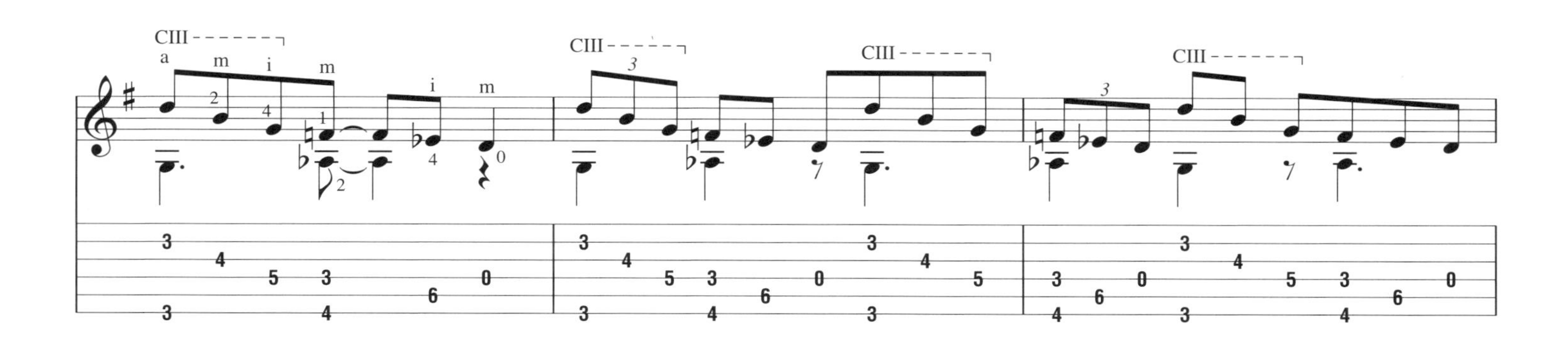
CIII
CIII
CIII
CIII

CI
ord.
H.H.
H.H.

f
*sustained
*next 4 meas.

Moderately fast ♩ = 144
mf

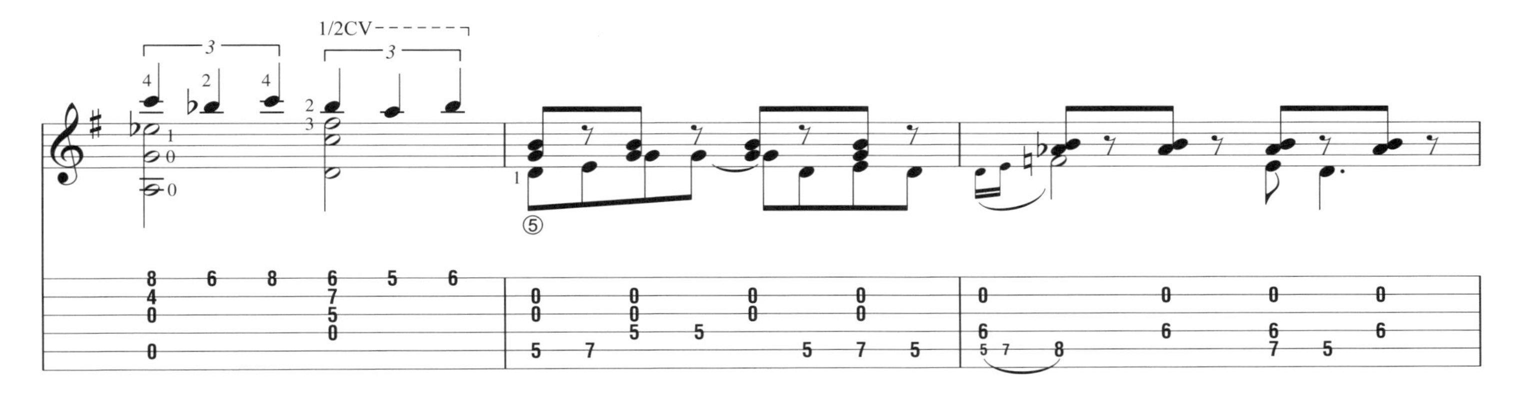
1/2CV

5/6CVIII

5/6CVIII

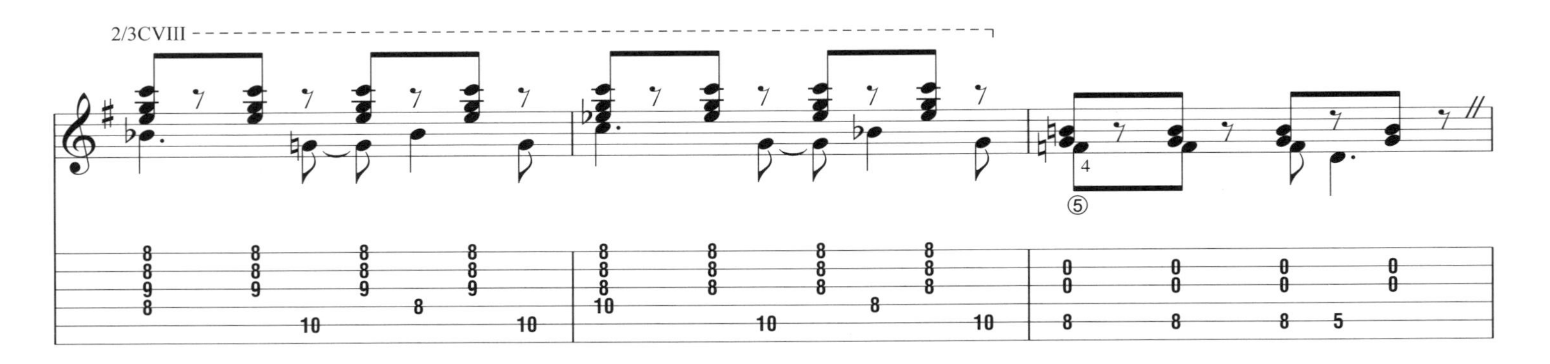
2/3CVIII

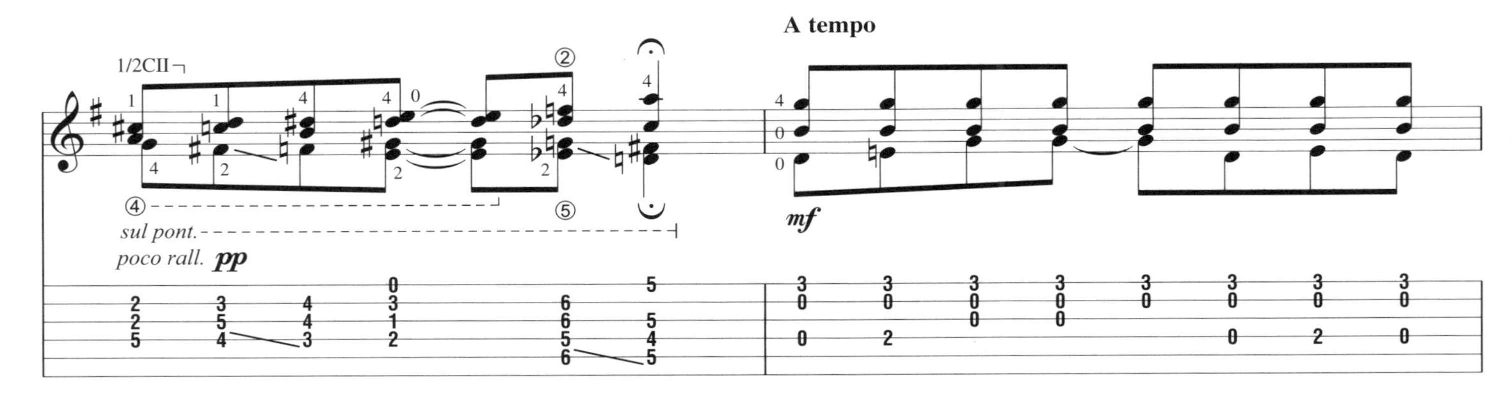
1/2CII
A tempo
sul pont.
poco rall.
pp
mf

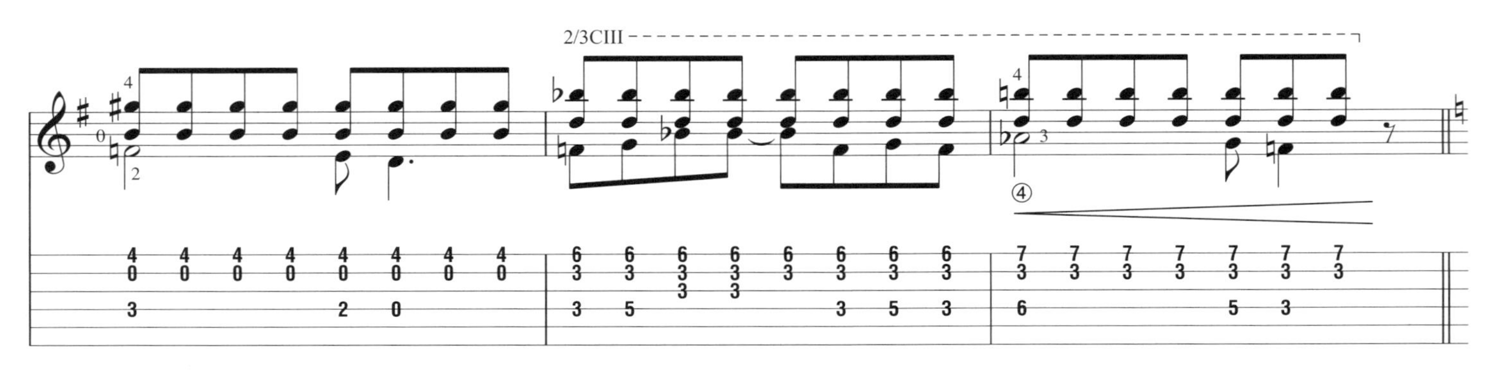
2/3CIII

agitated

2/3CI
H.H.
ord.

2/3CI
H.H.
2/3CVI

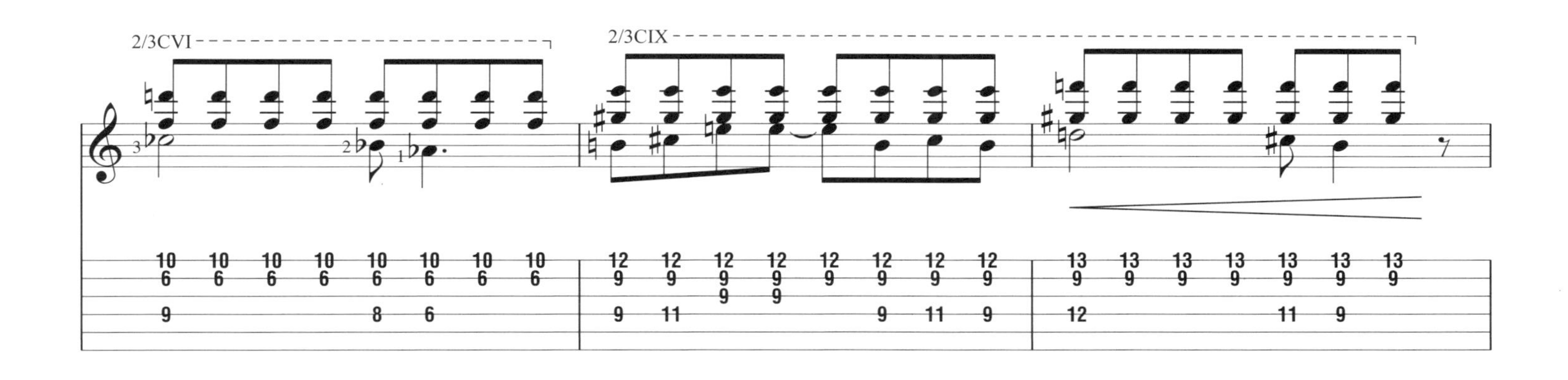
2/3CVI
2/3CIX

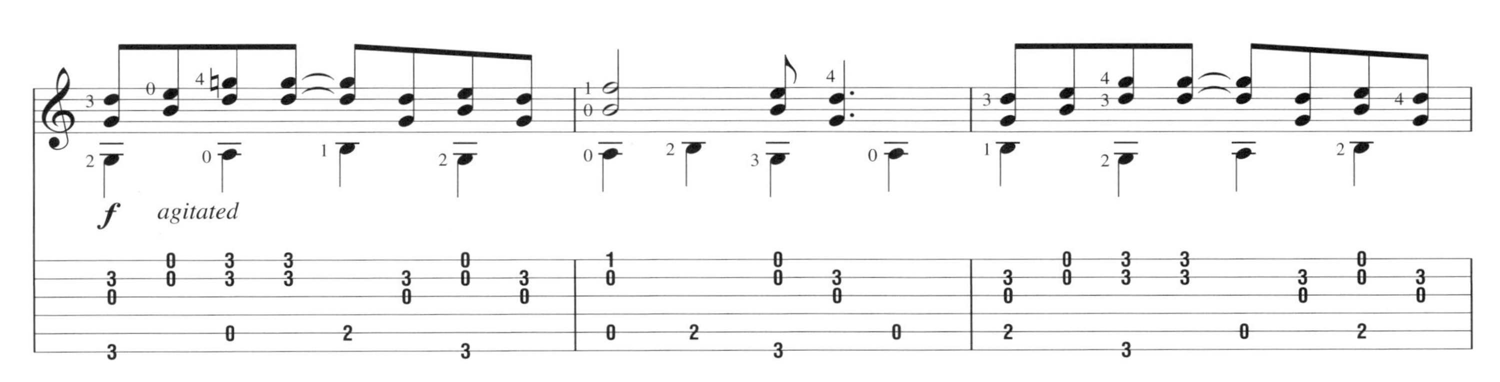
agitated

Cadenza
molto rit.
sim.
pp
let ring
Rubato
1/2CI
1/2CV
sul pont.
p
CVII
rall.
H.H.
Moderately slow ♩ = 80
VI H.B.
CII

CII
2/3CVI
VI H.B.
1/2CV
CIX
2/3CIX
CII
H.H.
CI
H.H.
rit.
A tempo
VI H.B.

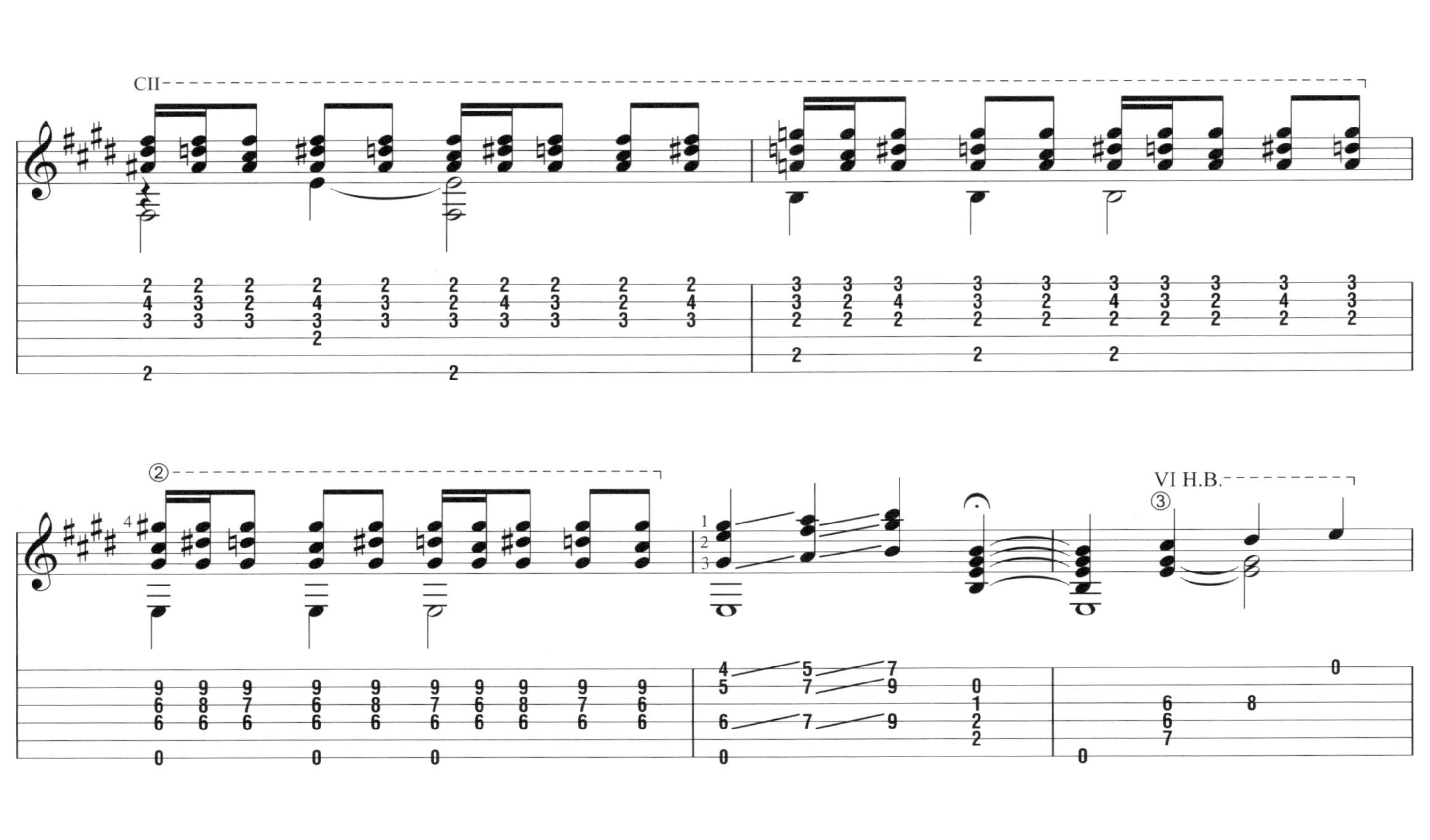
CII
VI H.B.

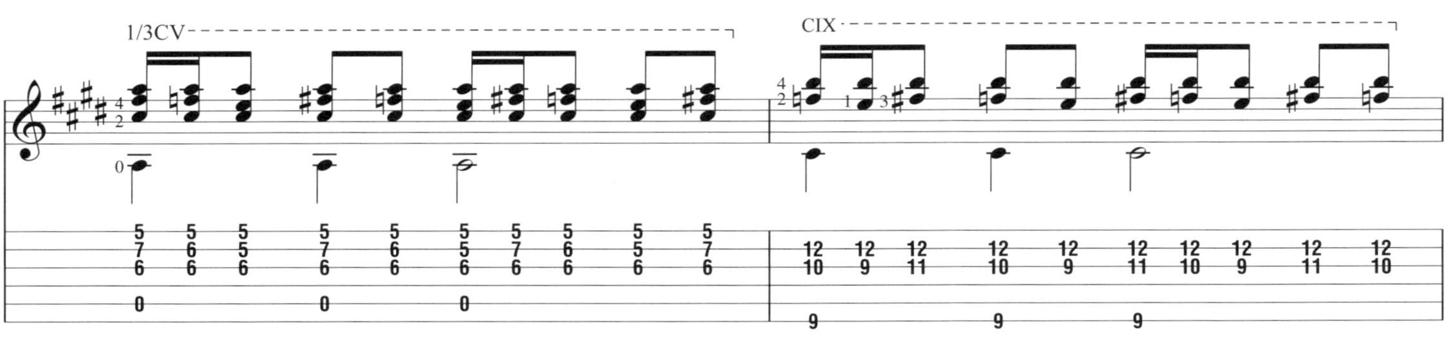
1/3CV
CIX

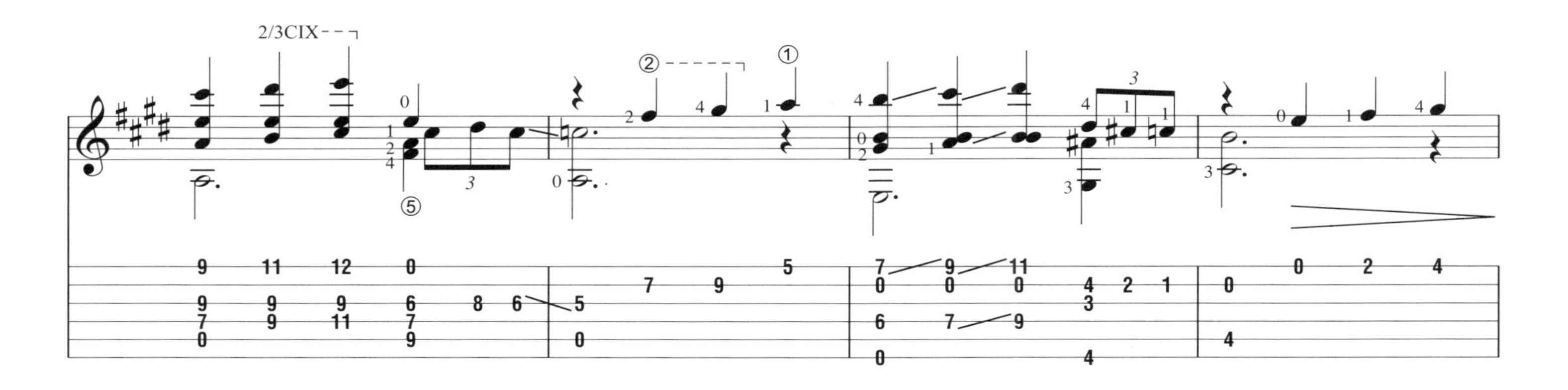
2/3CIX

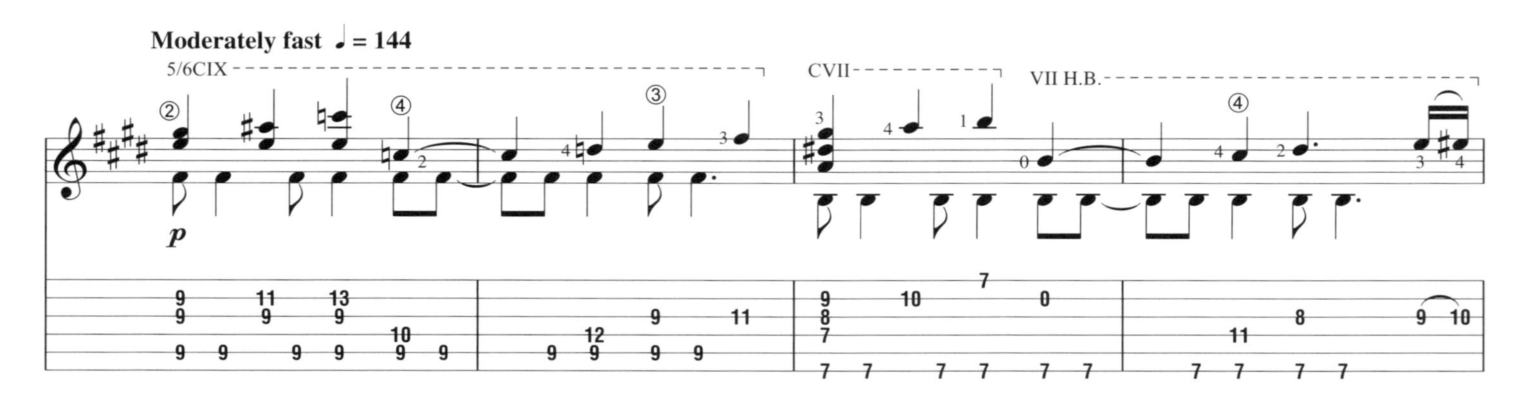
Moderately fast ♩ = 144
5/6CIX
CVII
VII H.B.

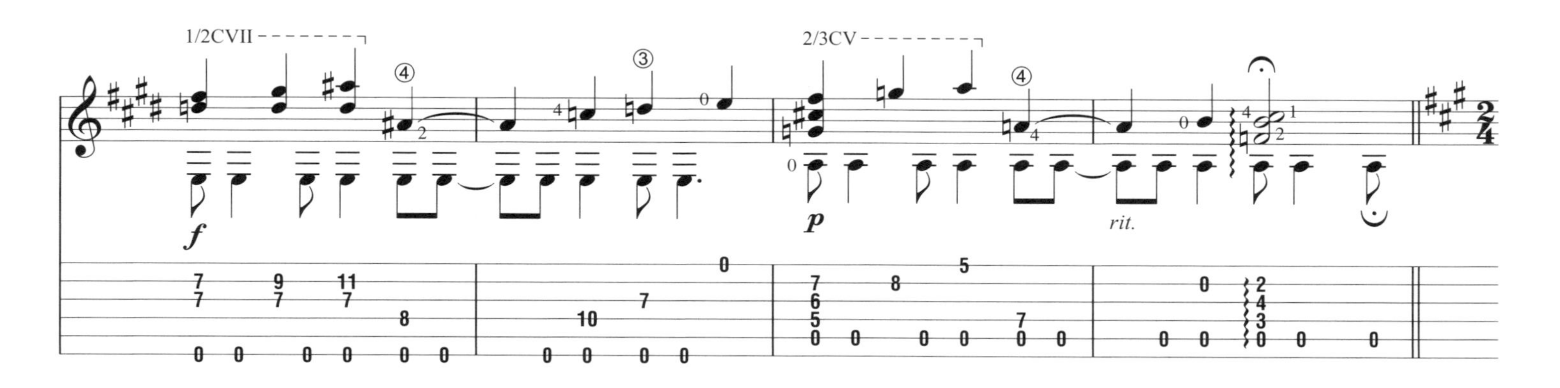
1/2CVII
2/3CV
f
p
rit.

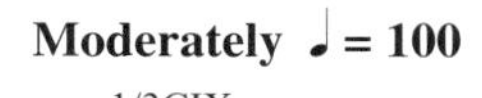
Moderately ♩ = 100

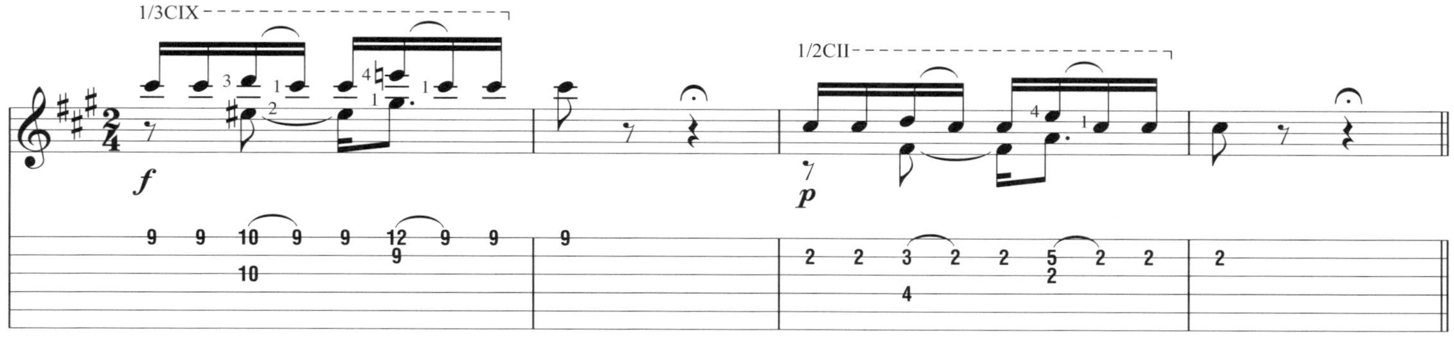
1/3CIX
1/2CII
f
p

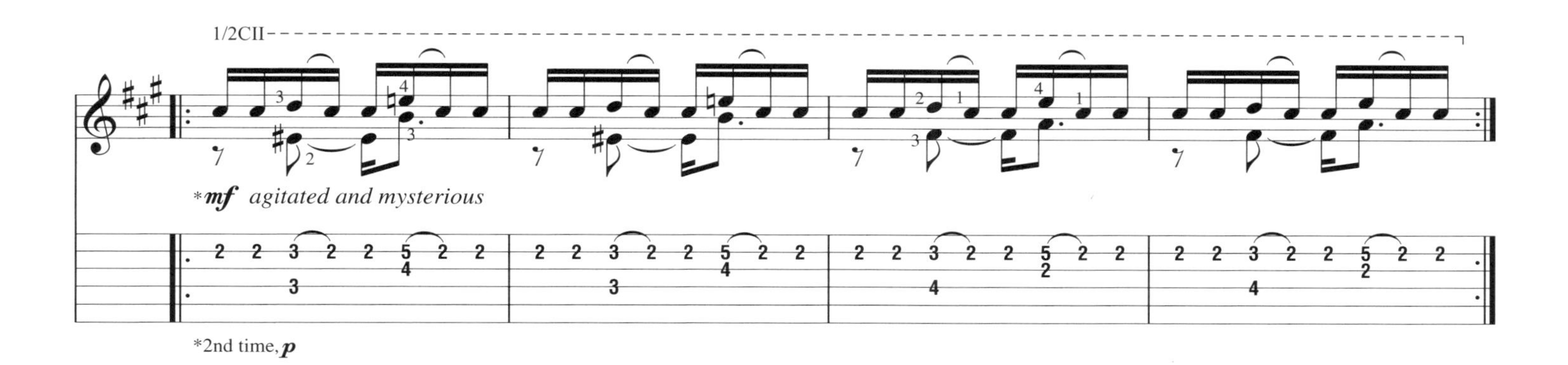
1/2CII
*mf agitated and mysterious
*2nd time, p

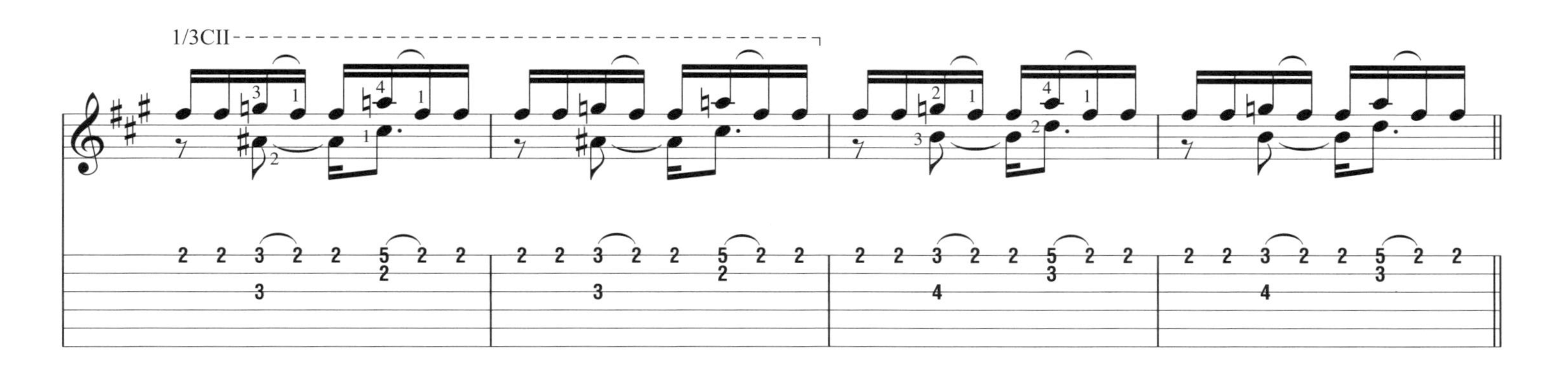
1/3CII

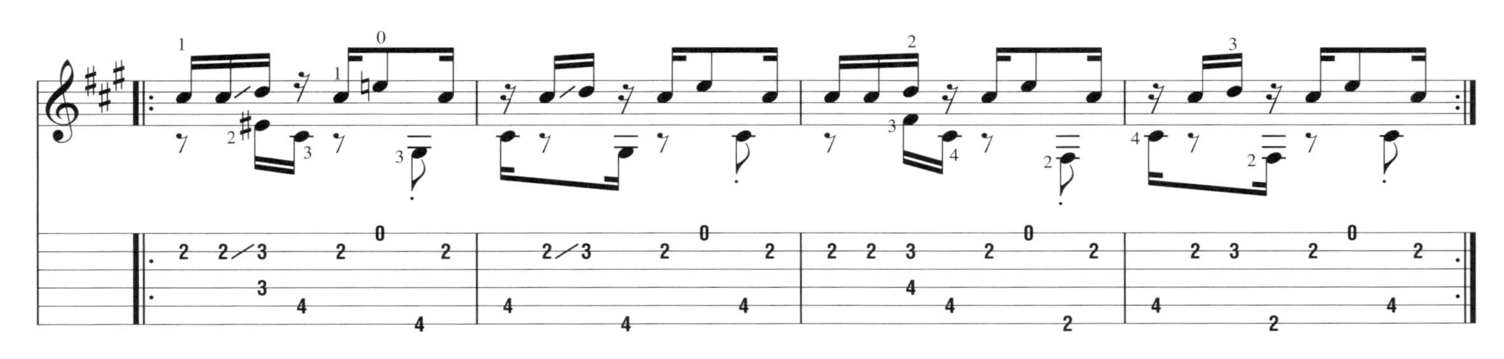

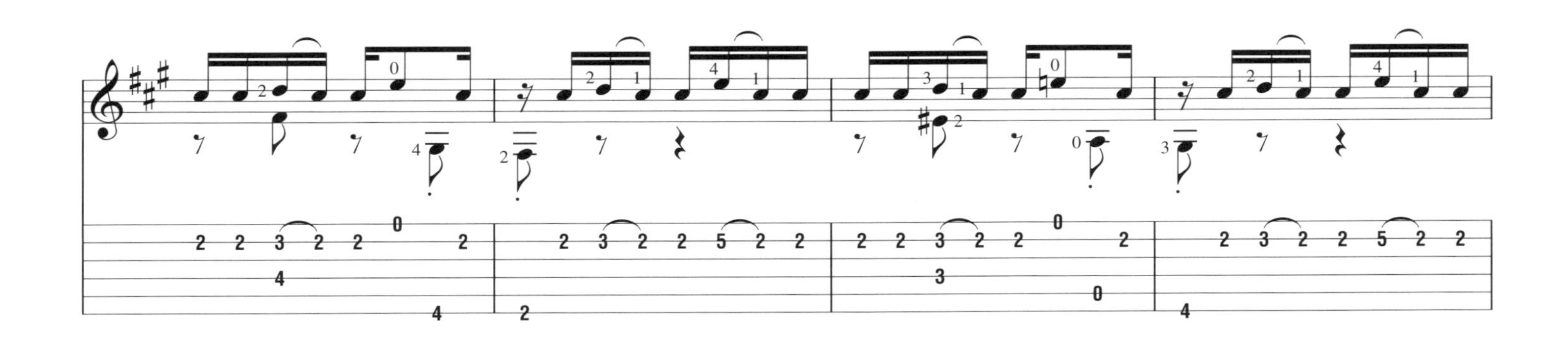

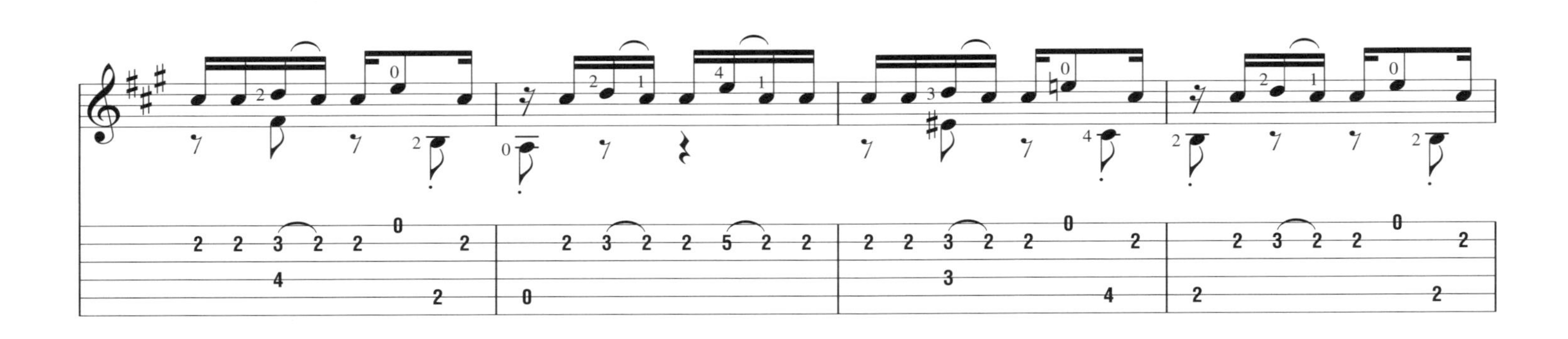

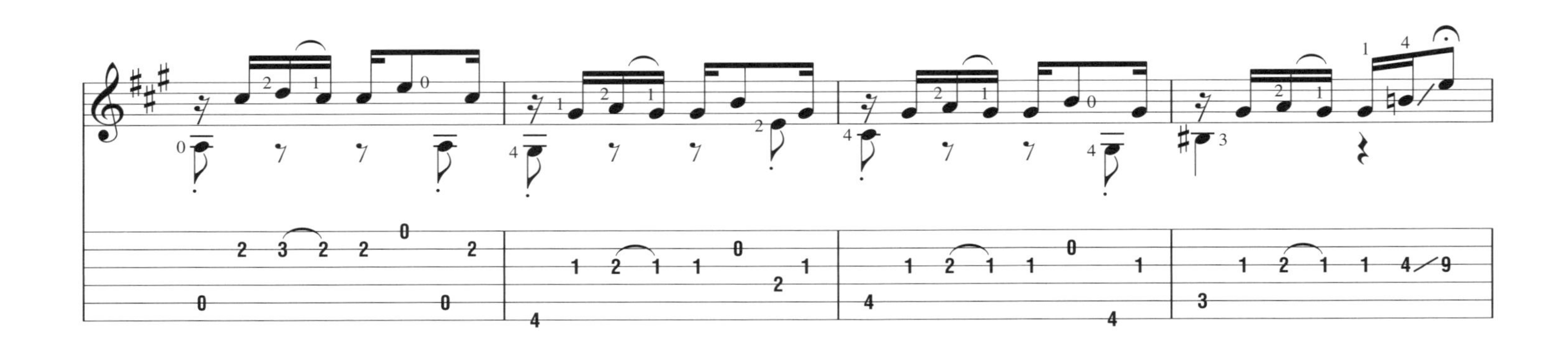

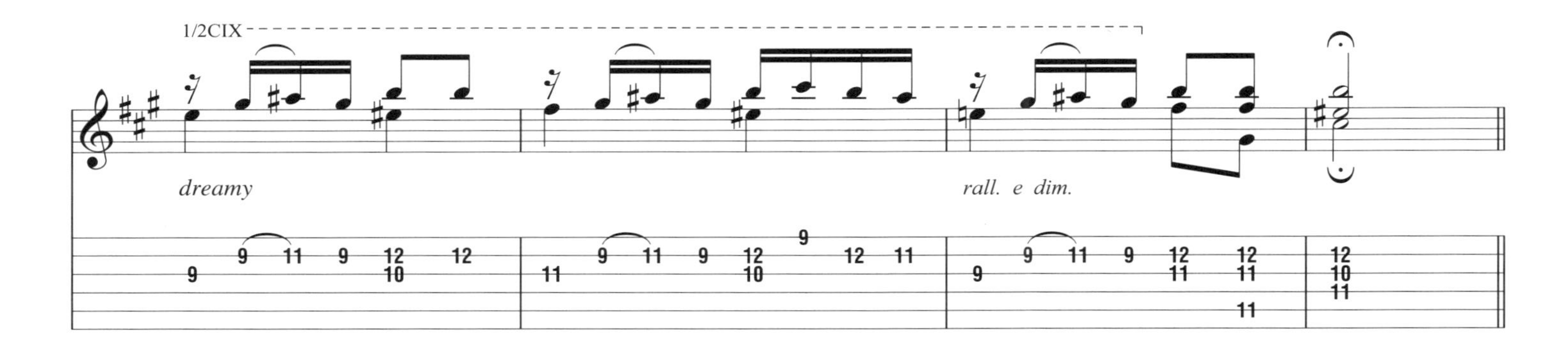
1/2CIX
dreamy
rall. e dim.

Moderately fast ♩ = 144
2/3CVI
p
let ring
H.H.

2/3CVI
H.H.
let ring

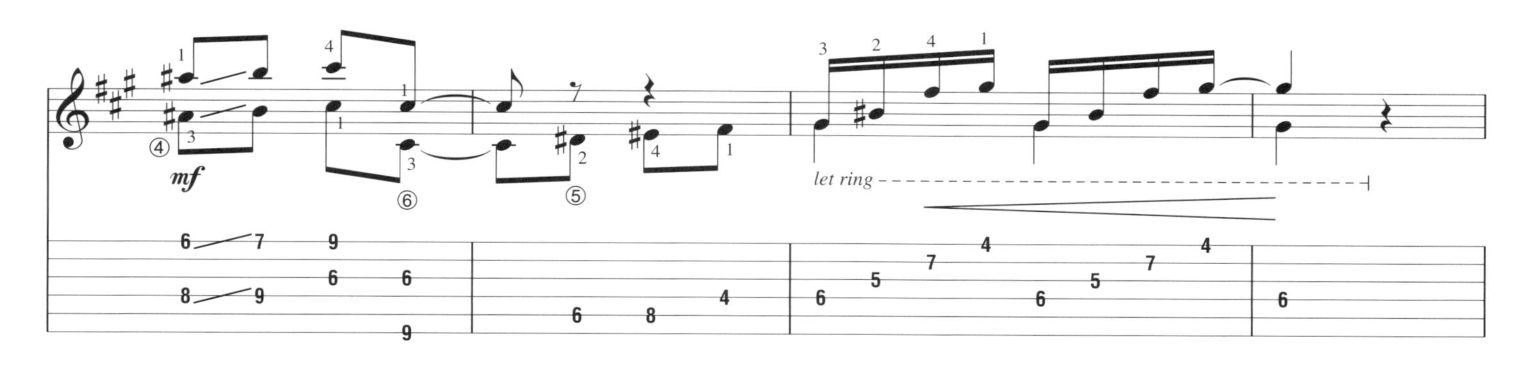
mf
let ring

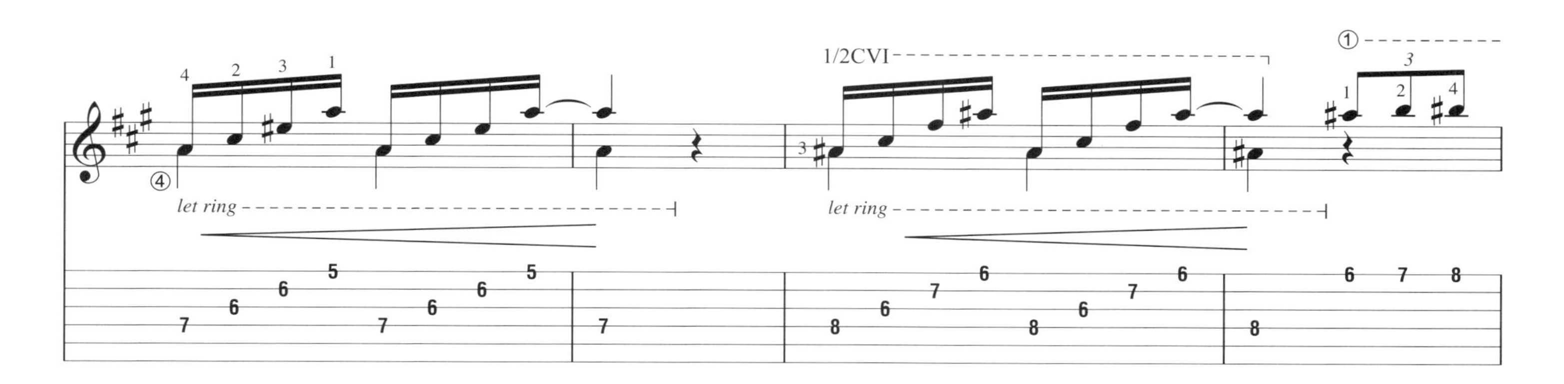
let ring
1/2CVI
let ring

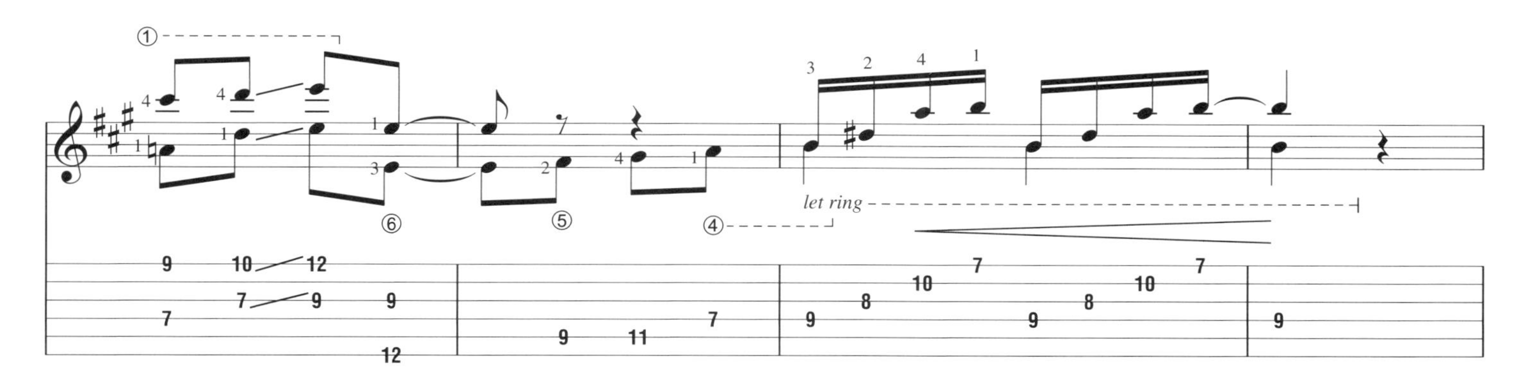
let ring

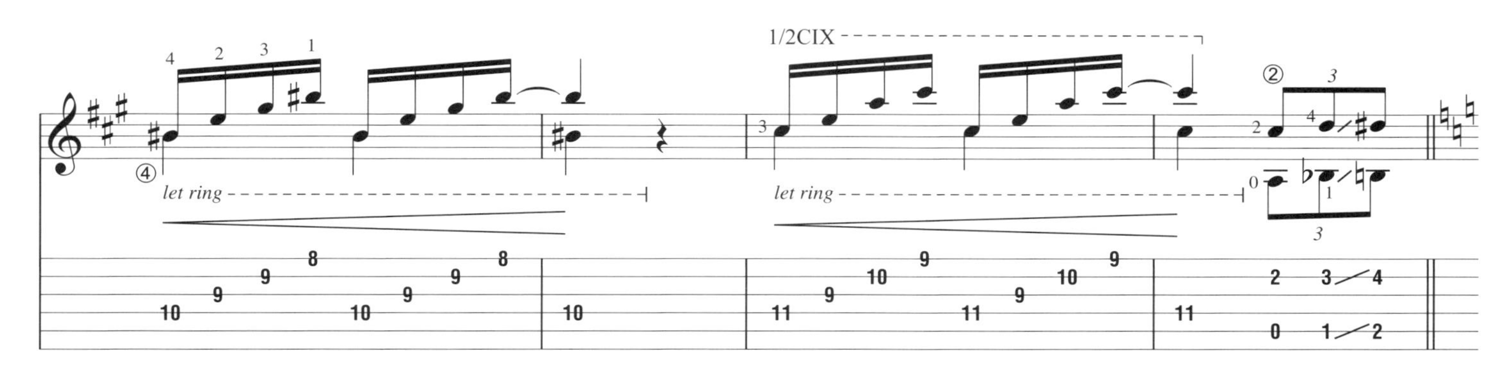
let ring
1/2CIX
let ring

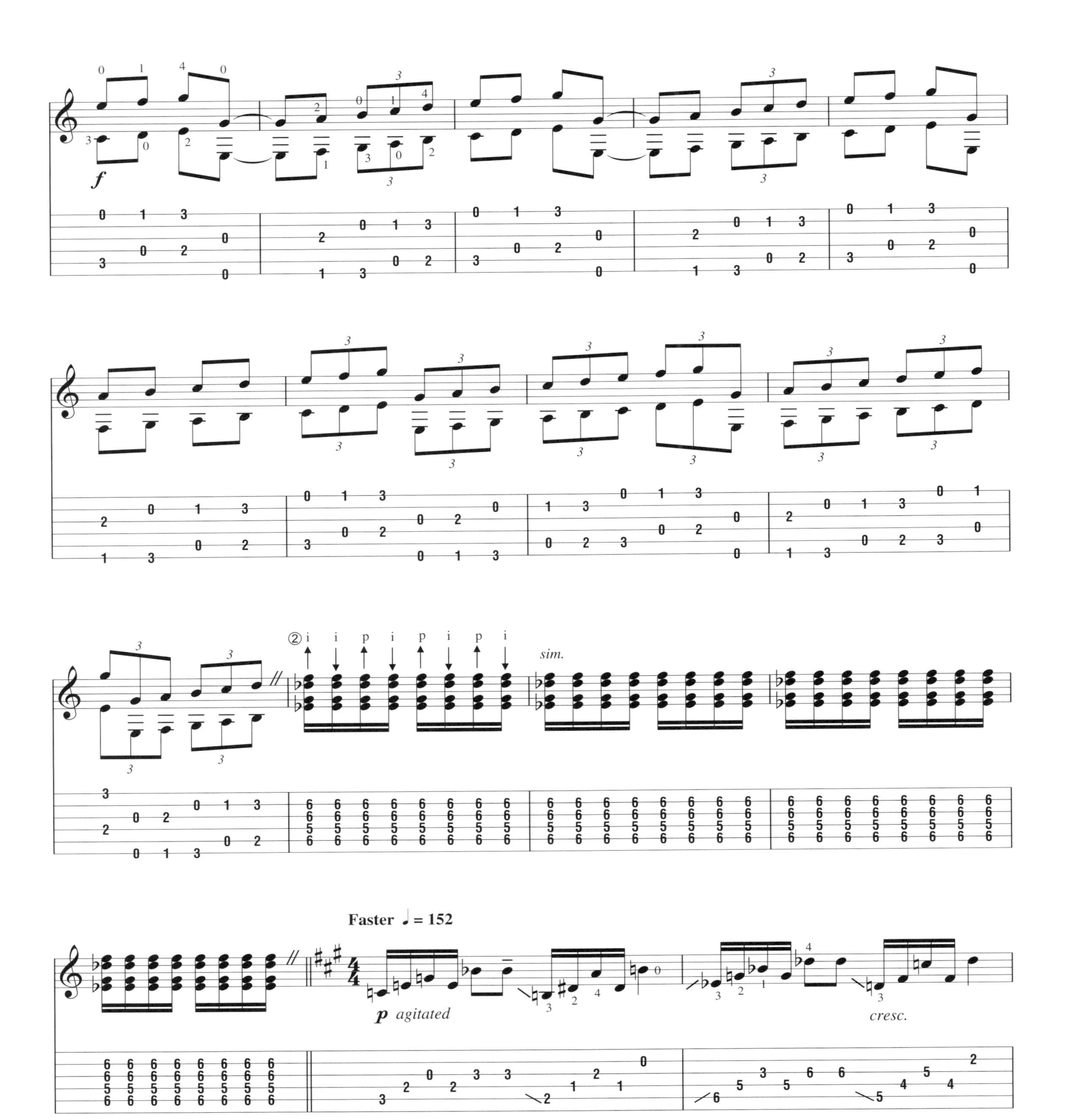
f
sim.
Faster ♩ = 152
p agitated
cresc.

5/6CIV

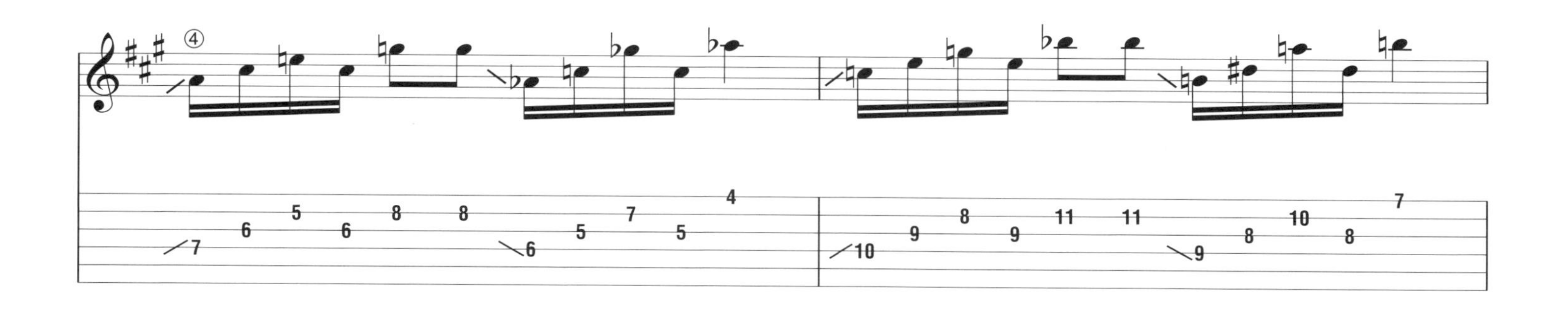

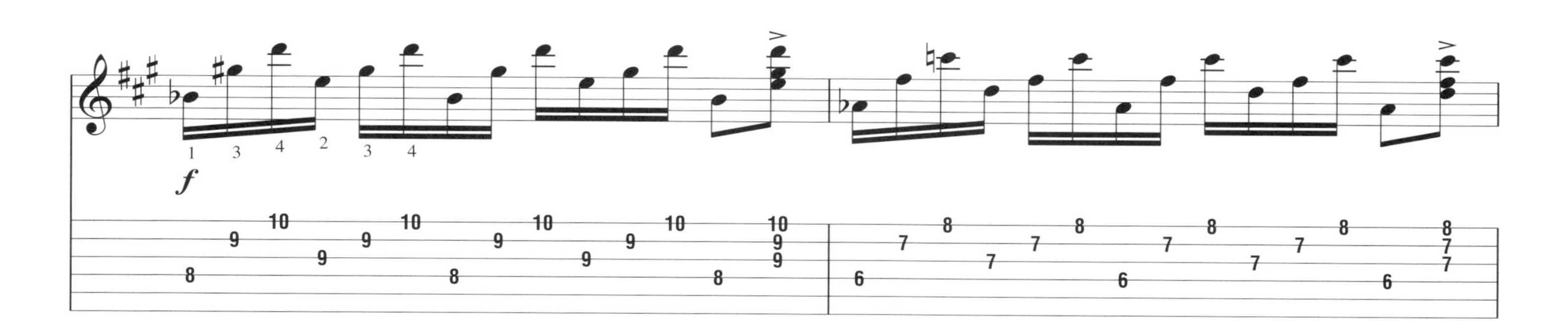

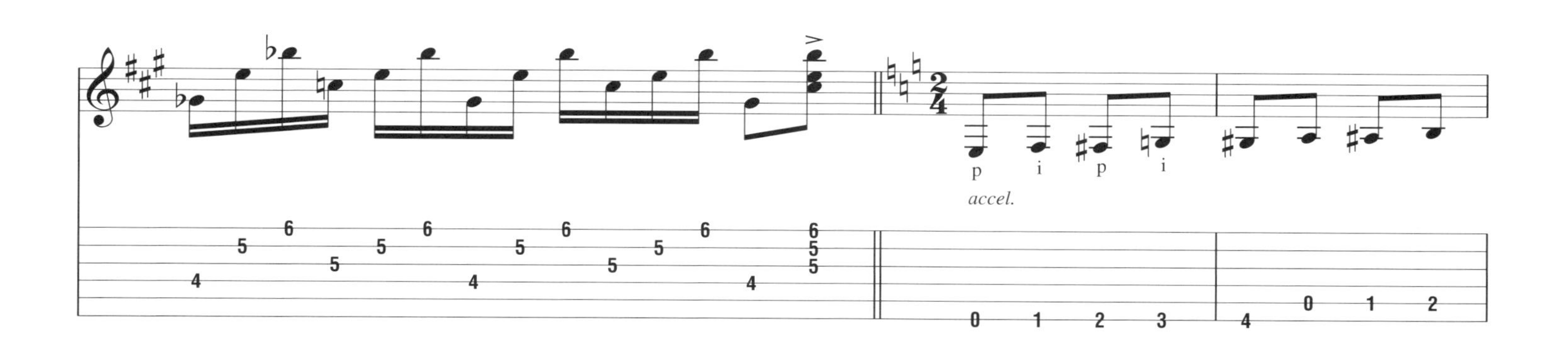
accel.

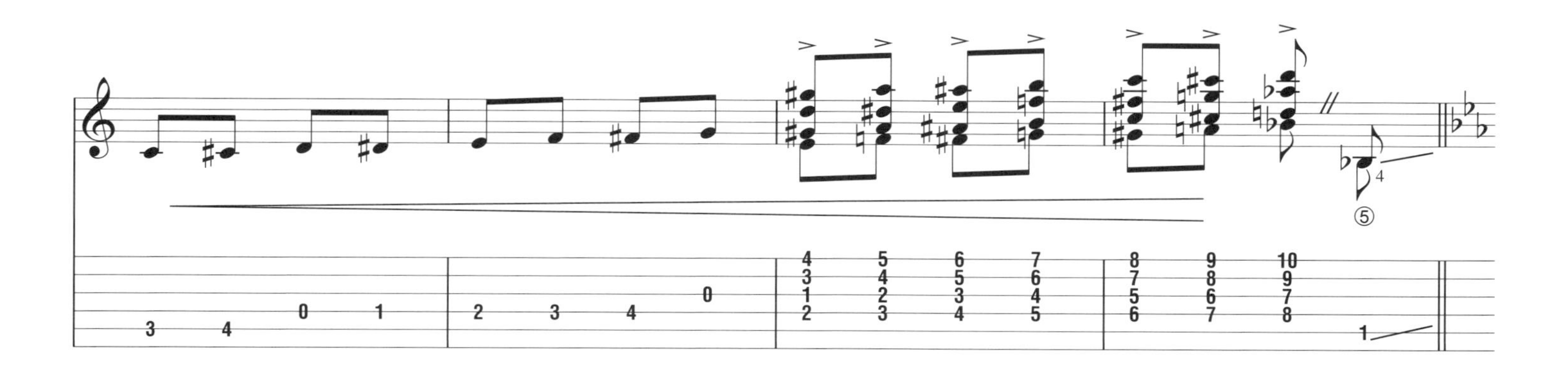

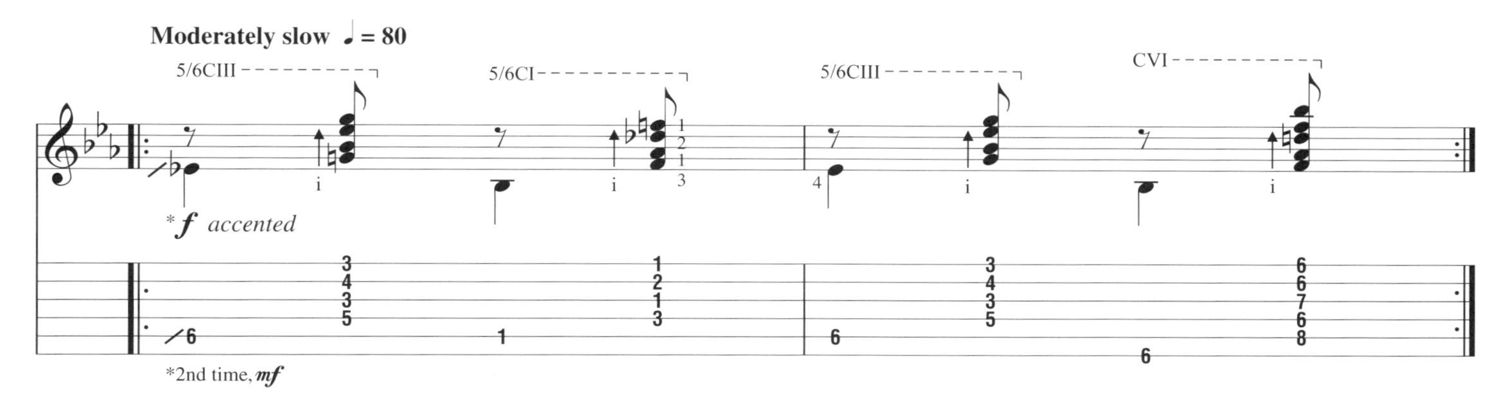
Moderately slow ♩ = 80
5/6CIII
5/6CI
5/6CIII
CVI
*f accented
*2nd time, mf

CVI
CVI
mf grandiose
CVI
CVI
CVI
CIV
p
CIV

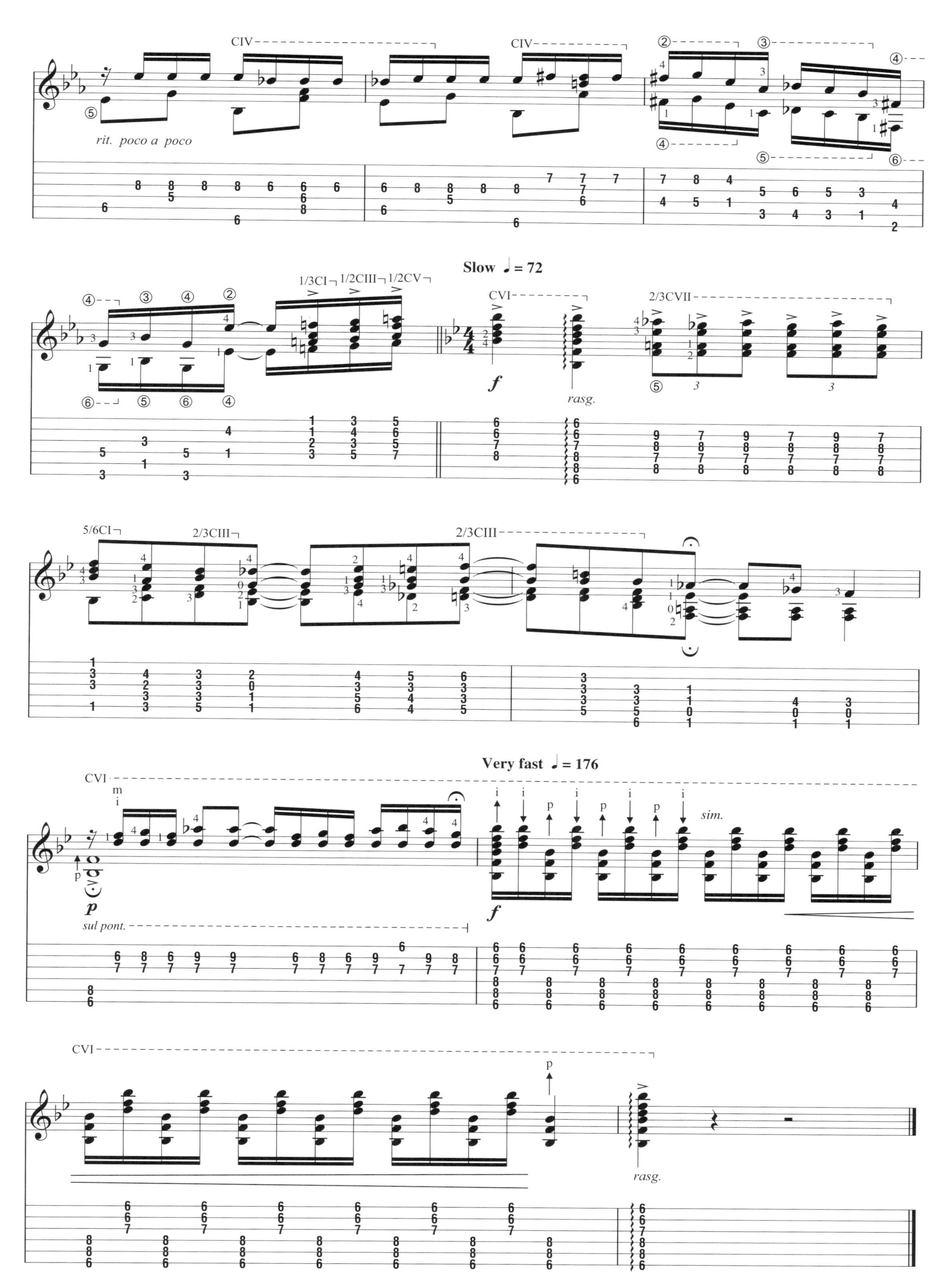
CIV
CIV
rit. poco a poco
Slow ♩ = 72
1/3CI
1/2CIII
1/2CV
CVI
2/3CVII
rasg.
5/6CI
2/3CIII
2/3CIII
Very fast ♩ = 176
CVI
sim.
sul pont.
CVI
rasg.

CLASSICAL GUITAR

PUBLICATIONS FROM HAL LEONARD

THE BEATLES FOR CLASSICAL GUITAR

Includes 20 solos from big Beatles hits arranged for classical guitar, complete with left-hand and right-hand fingering. Songs include: All My Loving • And I Love Her • Can't Buy Me Love • Fool on the Hill • From a Window • Hey Jude • If I Fell • Let It Be • Michelle • Norwegian Wood • Obla Di • Ticket to Ride • Yesterday • and more. Features arrangements and an introduction by Joe Washington, as well as his helpful hints on classical technique and detailed notes on how to play each song. The book also covers parts and specifications of the classical guitar, tuning, and Joe's "Strata System" – an easy-reading system applied to chord diagrams.

_______ 00699237 Classical Guitar $19.99

CZERNY FOR GUITAR

12 Scale Studies for Classical Guitar

by David Patterson

Adapted from Carl Czerny's *School of Velocity, Op. 299* for piano, this lesson book explores 12 keys with 12 different approaches or "treatments." You will explore a variety of articulations, ranges and technical perspectives as you learn each key. These arrangements will not only improve your ability to play scales fluently, but will also develop your ears, knowledge of the fingerboard, reading abilities, strength and endurance. In standard notation and tablature.

_______ 00701248 .... $9.99

MATTEO CARCASSI – 25 MELODIC AND PROGRESSIVE STUDIES, OP. 60

arr. Paul Henry

One of Carcassi's (1792-1853) most famous collections of classical guitar music – indispensable for the modern guitarist's musical and technical development. Performed by Paul Henry. 49-minute audio accompaniment.

_______ 00696506 Book/CD Pack $17.95

CLASSICAL & FINGERSTYLE GUITAR TECHNIQUES

by David Oakes • Musicians Institute

This Master Class with MI instructor David Oakes is aimed at any electric or acoustic guitarist who wants a quick, thorough grounding in the essentials of classical and fingerstyle technique. Topics covered include: arpeggios and scales, free stroke and rest stroke, P-i scale technique, three-to-a-string patterns, natural and artificial harmonics, tremolo and rasgueado, and more. The book includes 12 intensive lessons for right and left hand in standard notation & tab, and the CD features 92 solo acoustic tracks.

_______ 00695171 Book/CD Pack $17.99

CLASSICAL GUITAR CHRISTMAS COLLECTION

Includes classical guitar arrangements in standard notation and tablature for more than two dozen beloved carols: Angels We Have Heard on High • Auld Lang Syne • Ave Maria • Away in a Manger • Canon in D • The First Noel • God Rest Ye Merry, Gentlemen • Hark! the Herald Angels Sing • I Saw Three Ships • Jesu, Joy of Man's Desiring • Joy to the World • O Christmas Tree • O Holy Night • Silent Night • What Child Is This? • and more.

_______ 00699493 Guitar Solo $9.95

CLASSICAL GUITAR WEDDING

Perfect for players hired to perform for someone's big day, this songbook features 16 classsical wedding favorites arranged for solo guitar in standard notation and tablature. Includes: Air on the G String • Ave Maria • Bridal Chorus • Canon in D • Jesu, Joy of Man's Desiring • Minuet • Sheep May Safely Graze • Wedding March • and more.

_______ 00699563 Solo Guitar with Tab $10.95

CLASSICAL MASTERPIECES FOR GUITAR

27 works by Bach, Beethoven, Handel, Mendelssohn, Mozart and more transcribed with standard notation and tablature. Now anyone can enjoy classical material regardless of their guitar background. Also features stay-open binding.

_______ 00699312 .... $12.95

MASTERWORKS FOR GUITAR

Over 60 Favorites from Four Centuries
World's Great Classical Music

Dozens of classical masterpieces: Allemande • Bourree • Canon in D • Jesu, Joy of Man's Desiring • Lagrima • Malaguena • Mazurka • Piano Sonata No. 14 in C# Minor (Moonlight) Op. 27 No. 2 First Movement Theme • Ode to Joy • Prelude No. I (Well-Tempered Clavier).

_______ 00699503 .... $16.95

A MODERN APPROACH TO CLASSICAL GUITAR

by Charles Duncan

This multi-volume method was developed to allow students to study the art of classical guitar within a new, more contemporary framework. For private, class or self-instruction. Book One incorporates chord frames and symbols, as well as a recording to assist in tuning and to provide accompaniments for at-home practice. Book One also introduces beginning fingerboard technique and music theory. Book Two and Three build upon the techniques learned in Book One.

_______ 00695114 Book 1 – Book Only.............. $6.99
_______ 00695113 Book 1 – Book/CD Pack $10.99
_______ 00695116 Book 2 – Book Only.............. $6.99
_______ 00695115 Book 2 – Book/CD Pack $10.99
_______ 00699202 Book 3 – Book Only.............. $7.95
_______ 00695117 Book 3 – Book/CD Pack $10.95
_______ 00695119 Composite Book/CD Pack..... $29.99

ANDRES SEGOVIA – 20 STUDIES FOR GUITAR

Sor/Segovia

20 studies for the classical guitar written by Beethoven's contemporary, Fernando Sor, revised, edited and fingered by the great classical guitarist Andres Segovia. These essential repertoire pieces continue to be used by teachers and students to build solid classical technique. Features a 50-minute demonstration CD.

_______ 00695012 Book/CD Pack $18.95
_______ 00006363 Book Only $7.95

THE FRANCISCO TÁRREGA COLLECTION

edited and performed by Paul Henry

Considered the father of modern classical guitar, Francisco Tárrega revolutionized guitar technique and composed a wealth of music that will be a cornerstone of classical guitar repertoire for centuries to come. This unique book/CD pack features 14 of his most outstanding pieces in standard notation and tab, edited and performed on CD by virtuoso Paul Henry. Includes: Adelita • Capricho Árabe • Estudio Brillante • Grand Jota • Lágrima • Malagueña • María • Recuerdos de la Alhambra • Tango • and more, plus bios of Tárrega and Henry.

_______ 00698993 Book/CD Pack $19.99

HAL•LEONARD® CORPORATION
7777 W. Bluemound Rd. P.O. Box 13819 Milwaukee, WI 53213

Visit Hal Leonard Online at **www.halleonard.com**

IMPROVE YOUR IMPROV

AND OTHER JAZZ TECHNIQUES WITH BOOKS FROM HAL LEONARD

JAZZ GUITAR

HAL LEONARD GUITAR METHOD

by Jeff Schroedl

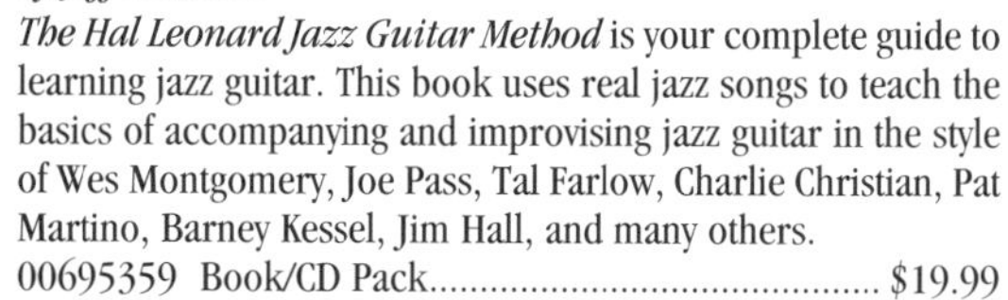

The Hal Leonard Jazz Guitar Method is your complete guide to learning jazz guitar. This book uses real jazz songs to teach the basics of accompanying and improvising jazz guitar in the style of Wes Montgomery, Joe Pass, Tal Farlow, Charlie Christian, Pat Martino, Barney Kessel, Jim Hall, and many others.

00695359 Book/CD Pack.. $19.99

AMAZING PHRASING

50 WAYS TO IMPROVE YOUR IMPROVISATIONAL SKILLS • *by Tom Kolb*

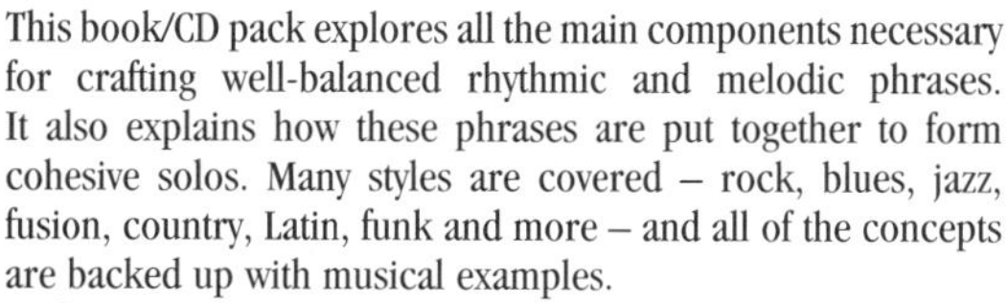

This book/CD pack explores all the main components necessary for crafting well-balanced rhythmic and melodic phrases. It also explains how these phrases are put together to form cohesive solos. Many styles are covered – rock, blues, jazz, fusion, country, Latin, funk and more – and all of the concepts are backed up with musical examples.

00695583 Book/CD Pack.. $19.95

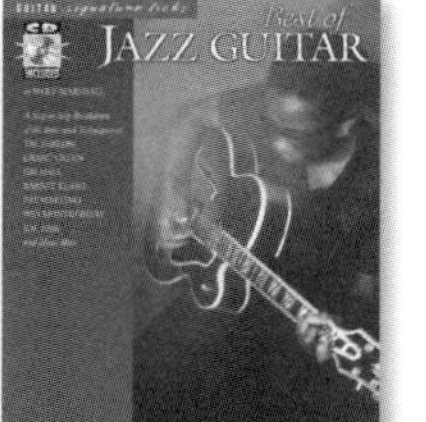

BEST OF JAZZ GUITAR

by Wolf Marshall • Signature Licks

In this book/CD pack, Wolf Marshall provides a hands-on analysis of 10 of the most frequently played tunes in the jazz genre, as played by the leading guitarists of all time. Each selection includes technical analysis and performance notes, biographical sketches, and authentic matching audio with backing tracks.

00695586 Book/CD Pack.. $24.95

CHORD-MELODY PHRASES FOR GUITAR

by Ron Eschete • REH ProLessons Series

Expand your chord-melody chops with these outstanding jazz phrases! This book covers: chord substitutions, chromatic movements, contrary motion, pedal tones, inner-voice movements, reharmonization techniques, and much more. Includes standard notation and tab, and a CD.

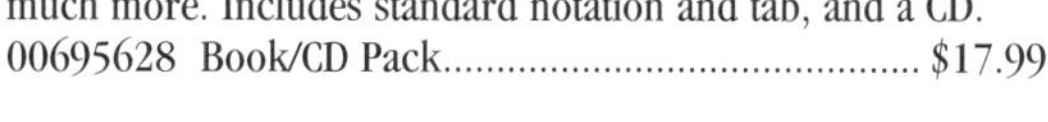

00695628 Book/CD Pack.. $17.99

CHORDS FOR JAZZ GUITAR

THE COMPLETE GUIDE TO COMPING, CHORD MELODY AND CHORD SOLOING • *by Charlton Johnson*

This book/CD pack will teach you how to play jazz chords all over the fretboard in a variety of styles and progressions. It covers: voicings, progressions, jazz chord theory, comping, chord melody, chord soloing, voice leading and many more topics. The CD includes 98 full-band demo tracks. No tablature.

00695706 Book/CD Pack.. $19.95

CRASH COURSE ON JAZZ GUITAR VOICINGS

THE ESSENTIAL GUIDE FOR ALL GUITARISTS

by Hugh Burns • Artemis Editions

This ultimate beginner's guide to jazz guitar covers: jazz harmony explained simply, easy essential jazz shapes to get you playing right away, classic jazz progressions, vamps, turnarounds and substitutions and more.

00695815 Book/CD Pack.. $9.95

FRETBOARD ROADMAPS – JAZZ GUITAR

THE ESSENTIAL GUITAR PATTERNS THAT ALL THE PROS KNOW AND USE • *by Fred Sokolow*

This book/CD pack will get guitarists playing lead & rhythm anywhere on the fretboard, in any key! It teaches a variety of lead guitar styles using moveable patterns, double-note licks, sliding pentatonics and more, through easy-to-follow diagrams and instructions. The CD includes 54 full-demo tracks.

00695354 Book/CD Pack.. $14.95

JAZZ IMPROVISATION FOR GUITAR

by Les Wise • REH ProLessons Series

This book/CD will allow you to make the transition from playing disjointed scales and arpeggios to playing melodic jazz solos that maintain continuity and interest for the listener. Topics covered include: tension and resolution, major scale, melodic minor scale, and harmonic minor scale patterns, common licks and substitution techniques, creating altered tension, and more! Features standard notation and tab, and a CD.

00695657 Book/CD Pack.. $16.95

JAZZ RHYTHM GUITAR

THE COMPLETE GUIDE

by Jack Grassel

This book/CD pack will help rhythm guitarists better understand: chord symbols and voicings, comping styles and patterns, equipment, accessories and set-up, the fingerboard, chord theory, and much more. The accompanying CD includes 74 full-band tracks.

00695654 Book/CD Pack.. $19.95

JAZZ SOLOS FOR GUITAR

LEAD GUITAR IN THE STYLES OF TAL FARLOW, BARNEY KESSEL, WES MONTGOMERY, JOE PASS, JOHNNY SMITH

by Les Wise

Examine the solo concepts of the masters with this book including phrase-by-phrase performance notes, tips on arpeggio substitution, scale substitution, tension and resolution, jazz-blues, chord soloing, and more. The CD includes full demonstration and rhythm-only tracks.

00695447 Book/CD Pack.. $17.95

101 MUST-KNOW JAZZ LICKS

A QUICK, EASY REFERENCE GUIDE FOR ALL GUITARISTS • *by Wolf Marshall*

Here are 101 definitive licks, plus a demonstration CD, from every major jazz guitar style, neatly organized into easy-to-use categories. They're all here: swing and pre-bop, bebop, post-bop modern jazz, hard bop and cool jazz, modal jazz, soul jazz and postmodern jazz. Includes an introduction, tips for using the book/CD, and a list of suggested recordings.

00695433 Book/CD Pack.. $17.95

SWING AND BIG BAND GUITAR

FOUR-TO-THE-BAR COMPING IN THE STYLE OF FREDDIE GREEN • *by Charlton Johnson*

This unique package teaches the essentials of swing and big band styles, including chord voicings, inversions, substitutions; time and groove, reading charts, chord reduction, and expansion; sample songs, patterns, progressions, and exercises; chord reference library; and a CD with over 50 full-demo examples. Uses chord grids – no tablature.

00695147 Book/CD Pack.. $19.99

FOR MORE INFORMATION, SEE YOUR LOCAL MUSIC DEALER, OR WRITE TO:

7777 W. BLUEMOUND RD. P.O. BOX 13819 MILWAUKEE, WI 53213

Visit Hal Leonard Online at **www.halleonard.com**

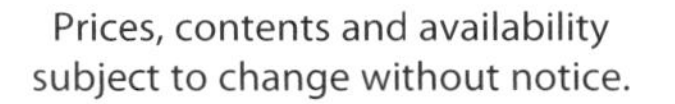

0710

THE PUBLICATIONS OF

CHRISTOPHER PARKENING

CHRISTOPHER PARKENING – DUETS AND CONCERTOS

Throughout his career, Christopher Parkening has had the opportunity to perform with many of the world's leading artists and orchestras, and this folio contains many selections from those collaborations. All of the pieces included here have been edited and fingered for the guitar by Christopher Parkening himself.
00690938 .... $24.99

THE CHRISTOPHER PARKENING GUITAR METHOD, VOL. 1 – REVISED

in collaboration with
Jack Marshall and David Brandon

Learn the art of the classical guitar with this premier method for beginners by one of the world's preeminent virtuosos and the recognized heir to the legacy of Andrés Segovia. Learn basic classical guitar technique by playing beautiful pieces of music, including over 50 classical pieces, 26 exercises, and 14 duets. Includes notes in the first position, how to hold the guitar, tuning, right and left hand technique, arpeggios, tone production, placement of fingers and nails, flats, naturals, key signatures, the bar, and more. Also includes many helpful photos and illustrations, plus sections on the history of the classical guitar, selecting a guitar, guitar care, and more.
00695228 .... $12.95

THE CHRISTOPHER PARKENING GUITAR METHOD, VOL. 2

Intermediate to Upper-Intermediate Level

Continues where Vol. 1 leaves off. Teaches: all notes in the upper position; tone production; advanced techniques such as tremolo, harmonics, vibrato, pizzicato and slurs; practice tips; stylistic interpretation; and more. The first half of the book deals primarily with technique, while the second half of the book applies the technique with repertoire pieces. As a special bonus, this book includes 32 previously unpublished Parkening edition pieces by composers including Dowland, Bach, Scarlatti, Sor, Tarrega and other, plus three duets for two guitars.
00695229 .... $12.95

PARKENING AND THE GUITAR – VOL. 1

Music of Two Centuries:
Popular New Transcriptions for Guitar
Virtuoso Music for Guitar

Ten transcriptions for solo guitar of beautiful music from many periods and styles, edited and fingered by Christopher Parkening. All pieces are suitable for performance by the advanced guitarist. Ten selections: Afro-Cuban Lullaby • Empress of the Pagodes (Ravel) • Menuet (Ravel) • Minuet in D (Handel) • Passacaille (Weiss) • Pastourelle (Poulenc) • Pavane for a Dead Princess (Ravel) • Pavane for a Sleeping Beauty (Ravel) • Preambulo (Scarlatti-Ponce) • Sarabande (Handel).
00699105 .... $9.95

PARKENING AND THE GUITAR – VOL. 2

Music of Two Centuries: Popular New Transcriptions for Guitar
Virtuoso Music for Guitar

Nine more selections for the advanced guitarist: Clair de Lune (Debussy) • Giga (Visée) • The Girl with the Flaxen Hair (Debussy) • Gymnopedie Nos. I-III (Satie) • The Little Shepherd (Debussy) • The Mysterious Barricades (Couperin) • Sarabande (Debussy).
00699106 .... $9.95

CHRISTOPHER PARKENING – ROMANZA

Virtuoso Music for Guitar

Three wonderful transcriptions edited and fingered by Parkening: Catalonian Song • Rumores de la Caleta • Romance.
00699103 .... $7.95

CHRISTOPHER PARKENING – SACRED MUSIC FOR THE GUITAR, VOL. 1

Seven inspirational arrangements, transcriptions and compositions covering traditional Christian melodies from several centuries. These selections appear on the Parkening album Sacred Music for the Guitar. Includes: Präludium (Bach) • Our Great Savior • God of Grace and God of Glory (2 guitars) • Brethren, We Have Met to Worship • Deep River • Jesus, We Want to Meet • Evening Prayer.
00699095 .... $10.95

CHRISTOPHER PARKENING – SACRED MUSIC FOR THE GUITAR, VOL. 2

Seven more selections from the album *Sacred Music for the Guitar*: Hymn of Christian Joy (guitar and harpsichord) • Simple Gifts • Fairest Lord Jesus • Stir Thy Church, O God Our Father • All Creatures of Our God and King • Glorious Things of Thee Are Spoken • Praise Ye the Lord (2 guitars).
00699100 .... $10.95

CHRISTOPHER PARKENING – SOLO PIECES

Sixteen transcriptions for solo guitar edited and fingered by Parkening, including: Allegro • Danza • Fugue • Galliard • I Stand at the Threshold • Prelude • Sonata in D • Suite Española • Suite in D Minor • and more.
00690939 .... $19.95

PARKENING PLAYS BACH

Virtuoso Music for Guitar

Nine transcriptions edited and fingered by Parkening: Preludes I, VI & IX • Gavottes I & II • Jesu, Joy of Man's Desiring • Sheep May Safely Graze • Wachet Auf, Ruft Uns Die Stemme • Be Thou with Me • Sleepers Awake (2 guitars).
00699104 .... $9.95

FOR MORE INFORMATION, SEE YOUR LOCAL MUSIC DEALER, OR WRITE TO:

7777 W. BLUEMOUND RD. P.O. BOX 13819 MILWAUKEE, WI 53213

Prices, contents and availability subject to change without notice.

1108